IMAGES OF WAR

SOPWITH CAMELS OVER ITALY 1917–1918

IMAGES OF WAR

SOPWITH CAMELS OVER ITALY 1917–1918

RARE PHOTOGRAPHS FROM WARTIME ARCHIVES

NORMAN FRANKS

Pen & Sword
AVIATION

First published in Great Britain in 2018 by
Pen & Sword Aviation
an imprint of
Pen & Sword Books Ltd
47 Church Street
Barnsley
South Yorkshire
S70 2AS

ISBN 978 1 52672 308 6

Typeset in 12/14 Gill Sans by
Aura Technology and Software Services, India

Printed and bound by CPI Group (UK) Ltd, Croydon, CR0 4YY

Pen & Sword Books Ltd incorporates the imprints of
Pen & Sword Archaeology, Atlas, Aviation, Battleground, Discovery, Family History, History, Maritime, Military, Naval, Politics, Railways, Select, Social History, Transport, True Crime, and Claymore Press, Frontline Books, Leo Cooper, Praetorian Press, Remember When, Seaforth Publishing and Wharncliffe.

For a complete list of Pen & Sword titles please contact
Pen & Sword Books Limited
47 Church Street, Barnsley, South Yorkshire, S70 2AS, England
E-mail: enquiries@pen-and-sword.co.uk
Website: www.pen-and-sword.co.uk

Contents

Chapter 1

War on the Italian Front

While Britain, France, Belgium and Germany were fighting massive battles on the Western Front in France, there were other actions going on in other parts of the world, such as the Russian Front, in the Middle East and in the mountainous regions of northern Italy, bordering Austria.

The Austro-Hungarian Empire had sided with Germany during the First World War, while Italy had been persuaded to become allied with Britain. Fighting between Italy and the Austro-Hungarians had begun in 1915 but, like the Western Front, had soon become bogged down, not helped by the mountainous terrain and thus very low temperatures. Initially Italy had been part of a triple alliance with Germany and Austro-Hungary but had not declared war in 1914, especially as there was no love lost between Italy and the Austro-Hungarians since the Napoleonic Wars. Italy was courted by allied diplomats early in the First World War, opted out of the triple alliance in April 1915 and declared war on the Austro-Hungarians on 23 May.

In 1915 there began a long series of battles around the Isonzo area, north of Trieste, and while both sides had some limited success, by and large very little was achieved, just as with the war in France. These Isonzo battles continued into 1916, taking place roughly every three months. Austrian forces did try another area with the Battle of Asiago, east of Lake Garda, in March 1916 but this too came to an end without conclusion. By 1917, it was clear that Germany needed to send support to its ally in the summer of that year and on 24 October the Germans and Austrians launched the Battle of Caporetto, back on the eastern side of Italy, forcing the Italians back some 12 miles (19 km) to the Tagliamento River. This required Britain and France to send help too, in all three British and two French divisions between 1917 and 1918. Italy had some fifty-eight divisions against Austria's sixty-one and Germany's five. In 1918 Czechoslovakia, Romania and the USA gave support with a few regiments.

To help judge the ferocity of the battles, allied losses totalled 651,000 killed and nearly 1 million wounded against 404,000 killed and 1.2 million wounded in the Austro-Hungarian ranks.

Germany had sent men and equipment to help their Austro-Hungarian allies after the Isonzo battles, leaving them so exhausted that the front was in danger of collapse. The Germans sent 7 divisions, 540 guns, 216 mortars and around 100 aircraft.

Everything came under the command of a new 14th Army (14.*Armeeoberkommando* [AOK]) formed in September 1917, with its headquarters at Vittorio Veneto from November and concentrated between Tolmin and Bovec.

Three German Jastas (fighter squadrons) formed the fighter element, comprising Jastas 1, 31 and 39. These three became the units of *Jagdgruppe* 14, commanded by *Oberleutnant* Hans Kummetz, who was the *Staffelführer* of Jasta 1. When it arrived in Italy, Jasta 1 was based at Veldes am See, then Aviano and finally Passanerlo. Its final base became San Fior, north-east of Conegliano, just before Christmas.

In the meantime Jasta 31, commanded by *Leutnant* Alwin Thurm, also stayed at Veldes before moving to Udine and then Aviano. In mid-November it was based at San Giacomo, near Vittoria, just north of Conegliano. Jasta 39, commanded by *Leutnant* August Raben until 17 November, also based itself at San Giacomo. *Oberleutnant* Franz von Kerssenbrock took temporary command as Raben was slightly wounded on the 17th, but he returned in December, remaining as its *Staffelführer* until March 1918. All three Jastas were equipped with Albatros D.III and D.V Scouts. Jasta 39 were mostly up against Italian aircraft.

Britain and France also sent aircraft in order to support their forces, the Royal Flying Corps (RFC) sending two squadrons initially, No. 28 with Sopwith Camels and No. 34 with RE8 two-seater observation machines. These units arrived at Milan on 12 and 14 November respectively, and within forty-eight hours had set up home at Verona before moving to Grossa, north-west of Padua, six days later. The RE8s settled at Milazzo at first but by the end of the month were also at Grossa.

Commanding 28 Squadron was Major H.F. Glanville, its three flight commanders being Captains W.G. Barker MC, R.C. White MC and J. Grant-Smith. The squadron had not long been on active duty on the Western Front, having 'gone over' to France during October. It had had a few fights with German aircraft and achieved seven victories, three by Barker. Perhaps the 'powers that be' decided they were 'last in, first out' when asked to provide a fighter squadron for Italy.

Much the same might have been thought of No. 45 Squadron, which was also moved to Italy in October. Although it had been in France since October 1916, it had been a two-seater Sopwith 1½ Strutter outfit and had only converted to Camels in July. It was commanded by Major A.M. Miller DSO, famous for his earlier work in recruiting men for the RFC in South Africa. However, 45 Squadron had seen a good deal of action and claimed over fifty victories before moving to Italy. Its flight commanders were Captains M.B. Frew, J.C.B. Firth and N. Macmillan.

The third Camel squadron selected for Italy was No. 66, commanded by Major R. Gregory MC. Another former fighter unit flying Sopwith Pups, it had converted to Camels in October 1917. Senior flight commander was Captain T.V. Hunter, along with acting Captain R. Erskine. It also made its base at Milano, then Verona and finally Grossa in December.

The RFC's Italian fighter allies in the air had been mostly French Nieuport Scouts and some Spad VIIs but these were mostly replaced by Hanriot HDI fighters by the time the RFC Camels reached the front. Later in 1918, Spad XIIIs also made an appearance. At the time of Caporetto the Italians had fifteen *Squadriglia* (fighter squadrons), while the Austrians had some ten *Fliegerkompanies* or Fliks, each with eighteen aircraft, plus a number of two-seater bombing and reconnaissance units known as *Aufklarungs*. The opposition fighters comprised Hansa-Brandenburg D.Is and some Aviatik D.Is, but mainly German Albatros D.III Scouts built under licence by the Österreichische Flugzeugfabrik AG (Öffag). In 1918 the Phönix D.I and D.IIa began to be met in combat.

Initially the Camel pilots' task was to protect the RE8 crews engaged on reconnaissance, photography and artillery-directing duties. In addition, the RE8 crews were called upon to fly bombing missions and ground-attack sorties. Not surprisingly, the Camel pilots felt restricted in flying escort and it was not long before they began to carry 20lb Cooper bombs on ground-attack operations in between escorts.

First blood for the Camels came on 29 November, with Captain Billy Barker destroying an Albatros Scout near Treviso. Barker, a Canadian, had been a reconnaissance pilot earlier in the war and had already been awarded the Military Cross as an observer and then, becoming a pilot, returned to his old unit and earned a Bar to this decoration. Following a period as an instructor, he was sent to 28 Squadron which was in the process of forming, taking command of A Flight. This first victory in Italy was Barker's fourth, the luckless pilot being *Leutnant* Erwin Härtl of Jasta 1 who was wounded. Barker gained his fifth victory on 3 December, another Albatros, the pilot being *Leutnant* Franz von Kerssenbrock from Jasta 39, the Jasta's acting *Staffelführer*, who was killed. Barker then attacked and shot down a balloon, probably from BK10.

No. 66 Squadron opened its Italian account on 8 December, Second Lieutenant H.K. Boyson sending an Albatros D.III down 'out of control' ('ooc'). It was Howard Boyson's first claim. He was an American from Illinois, who had joined the RFC in Canada. His opponent is thought to have been another Jasta 39 pilot, *Leutnant* Rudolf Bertelsmeier, who was taken prisoner. Boyson was injured in a crash in January 1918 but returned in May, adding four more victories to his name.

Also on the 8th, 28 Squadron claimed three victories, Captain Grant-Smith destroying what he described as an Aviatik two-seater and sending a second down out of control. Lieutenant C.W. Middleton accounted for a third Aviatik. Jasta 1 got into a fight with 66 Squadron, *Oberleutnant* Kummetz shooting down Second Lieutenant J.A.M. Robertson (B4604), who became a prisoner. He was the first British airman lost in combat in the Italian campaign.

On the 9th, 66's Second Lieutenant T.R. Whitehead caused an Albatros to crash. Two days later Lieutenant J.H. Mitchell MC claimed another Albatros, while Grant-Smith bagged an Aviatik. John Gordon Smith Cheetham Grant-Smith came from Glenlivet, Scotland and had served in the infantry before moving to the RFC. He was the heir to the Glenlivet whisky company. He had already been credited with two victories in France with 70 Squadron, so had now become an ace. Grant-Smith returned to France and to his old squadron and gained a sixth victory but was badly wounded in action on 29 May 1918. He was being operated on that night in hospital but, tragically, was killed by a bomb dropped by a German aircraft. Jasta 39 lost *Vizefeldwebel* Fritz Schröder at 1330 hours over St. Michele.

John Hart Mitchell came from Hereford and had won the Military Cross with the Essex Regiment prior to joining the RFC. His first victory with 28 Squadron on 20 October was an Albatros that was attacking fellow pilot W.G. Barker! His victory on 8 December appears to have been from Flik 58D, an Austrian two-seater. 'Mitch' was shortly to become a flight commander.

A second RE8 squadron, No. 42, had been taken from France and arrived in Italy during December and would remain until March 1918, at which time the big German offensive in France necessitated its return to the Western Front.

Christmas 1917 on the Italian Front saw events that in later years had a variety of different computations as to what happened, often with incorrect dates and varying claims. On Christmas Day, the 25th, Barker, having proposed an attack on an enemy airfield, had asked for volunteers but there were few takers. Lieutenant H.B. Hudson, English-born but living in Montreal when war came, idolized Barker and stepped forward. The operation was not authorized by the CO; however, Barker and Hudson flew to an Austrian airfield but finding no aircraft in sight, proceeded to shoot up the hangars and other buildings. The target was never recorded but is assumed to have been San Fior, the home of *Fliegerabteilung* 204(A), although San Felice was noted in the records. Several hangars were damaged and no doubt casualties were suffered among ground crews.

This obviously infuriated the Austrians and Germans so much that they launched a reprisal attack on the following day, 26 December. Some thirty enemy aircraft headed for the British bases in the early morning, with a smaller force going over around noon. It appears that the hostile force was crewed by men still suffering hangovers from the previous day, for it was not very well co-ordinated and had no fighter escort. The airfield attacked was Istrana, not 28's Grossa, and bombing accuracy was certainly very poor. Even so, one British and five Italian mechanics were killed and others wounded.

Although 28 Squadron got some Camels into the air, the main antagonists against the Austrians were the Italians of the 76ª and 78ª *Squadriglia*. In all, some nine enemy machines were claimed shot down, eight being DFW CVs, with just one being shared with three pilots of 28 Squadron, Messrs A.G. Jarvis, P.G. Mulholland and O.W. Frayne. Another enemy machine was an AEG GIV that was also attacked by Captain Mitchell and two of the Italians, *Tenente* Silvio Scaroni and *Capitano* Antonio Riva of 78ª. Riva shared two of the claims for his second and third victories; Scaroni's claims were his eighth and ninth. The AEG came from the German Boghol 4, falling inside Italian lines and becoming G.128 in the allied numbering series of 'captured' aircraft. Initially 28 Squadron thought this to have been a Gotha bomber.

There was some debate about Barker's unauthorized raid with 'Steve' Hudson, for although the reprisal was to cost the enemy a number of aircraft, by stirring up the Austrians it had caused death and injury among ground personnel at Istrana.

The pilots of 66 Squadron had ended the year with four victories during the month of December: Lieutenants S. Stanger an Albatros 'ooc' on the 14th; J.M. Warnock an Albatros two-seater on the 15th; while M.A. Mowat and R. Erskine claimed an LVG two-seater and a D.III respectively on the 16th. Stan Stanger, another Canadian from Montreal, had spent two and a half years in the Canadian army and US National Guard. He would end the war with thirteen victories plus the MC and DFC, having moved across to 28 Squadron during 1918.

Barker shot down a balloon on the 29th, while Lieutenants C.M. McEwen and A.B. Cooper shared an Albatros Scout on the 30th. Cliff McEwen came from Manitoba, a graduate of the University of Saskatchewan. 'Black Mike', as he was known, was a 28 Squadron original and the Albatros was the first of his twenty-seven victories.

Camels of 45 Squadron had a successful action on the 31st, with two Albatros Scouts destroyed and two 'ooc' by Second Lieutenants R.J. Brownell, H.M. Moody and R.J. Dawes. The action was fought with Jasta 31 and their certain loss was *Leutnant* Alwin Thurm, who was killed. Thurm had scored his fifth victory the previous day, a balloon. His last three victories had all been balloons and he was attacking a French balloon near Asolo when 45 Squadron intervened. His Albatros D.III (4879/17) came down inside allied lines.

Leutnant Ernst Fr. von Stenglin of Jasta 1 claimed a victory on 30 December, it being referred to as a Camel in some reports but none were lost. German pilots often confused Camels with Italian Hanriot fighters. The fact that Stenglin also claimed a Spad VII of the Italian 71ª *Squadriglia* is perhaps a clue to this combat. Stenglin was credited with six victories but not all were confirmed.

Sopwith Camels of 45 Squadron at Istrana, Italy, with pilots in the foreground and ground mechanics lined up with the aircraft.

Captain Norman Macmillan MC, flight commander with 45 Squadron when it moved from France to Italy in October 1917. He had a total of nine victories by this time, flying both Sopwith 1½ Strutters and Camels. From Scotland, he had previously served with the Highland Light Infantry.

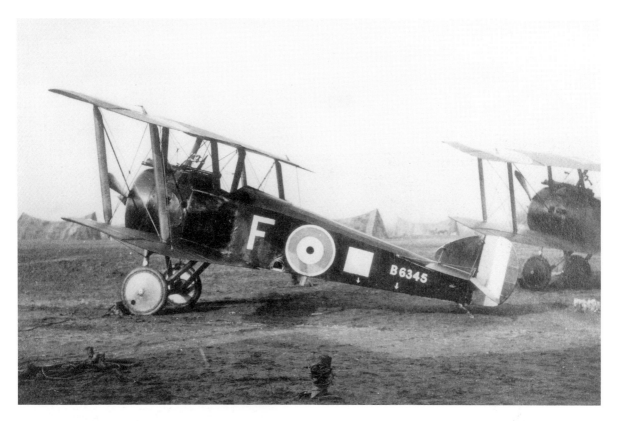

Sopwith Camel B6345 with 28 Squadron in Italy, October 1917. Flown by several pilots, it survived until it crashed on 20 April 1918. It was involved in the action fought on 26 December 1917, Second Lieutenant P.G. Mulholland sharing in the destruction of a DFW CV.

Captain J.C.B. Firth flew Strutters and Camels with 45 Squadron, claiming nine victories. He downed two more in Italy and received both the Military Cross and the Italian Bronze Medal for Military Valour. Originally with the 5th Battalion of the King's Shropshire Light Infantry, he was wounded on the first day of the Battle of Loos, 25 September 1915.

Above: Three flight commanders of 28 Squadron – Captains John Smith-Grant, Jim Mitchell and Billy Barker – outside a café at Gheddi with the waitresses. John Gordon Smith Cheetham Smith-Grant came from Glenlivet, Scotland, the eldest son of the late Colonel George Smith-Grant, and was heir to the Glenlivet whisky company. After service with the Royal Scots in 1915–16 he joined the RFC and was a two-seater pilot with 70 Squadron before moving to 28 as a flight commander. He gained his fifth victory on 10 December 1917. Returning to France and posted to 70 Squadron, he was tragically killed by a bomb while on the operating table in a field hospital on 29 May 1918, having been wounded in combat that day.

Opposite above: Four of 28 Squadron's pilots: Lieutenants C.M. McEwen; J.E. Hallonquist; J. Mackereth; S. Stanger. Except for Joe Mackereth who came from Essex, the other three were all Canadian. All four men distinguished themselves in Italy.

Opposite below: Captains J.H. Mitchell and W.G. Barker of 28 Squadron celebrating another successful combat action. James Hart Mitchell came from Hereford and had joined the RFC following service with the Essex Regiment. Canadian Billy Barker already had the MC and Bar for his service with observation squadrons in France before becoming a scout pilot in October 1917.

Above: Another picture outside the same café. Barker sits on the left, with Lieutenant P. Wilson to his left. Smith-Grant is next, P.G. Mulholland sits cross-legged in the foreground, and Jim Mitchell is on the far right smoking a cigarette.

Below: Billy Barker, H.B. Hudson and J.M. Mitchell standing in front of Barker's Camel B6313. Note the fur flying coat in contrast to Hudson's leather one. Mitchell again is snapped with a cigarette. Note also the flight leader's streamers attached to the wing struts. This Camel is B6313, famously used by Barker, so note the number one on the port wing and 45's white square on the starboard wing.

No. 28 Squadron's P.G. Mulholland, Jim Mitchell, Percy Wilson and an unknown pilot at Grossa airfield.

Lieutenant O.W. Frayne, a South African serving with 28 Squadron. He achieved four victories in Italy. However, he ran out of luck and petrol on 28 May 1918 and was injured in the subsequent crash-landing.

Lieutenant H.W. Morrison standing
by damaged Camel B5169 in which he
overturned on 4 May 1918. Lieutenant
C.M. McEwen claimed three victories in this
machine in early 1918 and would end the
war with a total of twenty-seven victories.

Portrait of James Mitchell MC, whose family
was from Yorkshire. By June 1918 he had
achieved eleven victories before returning
home in July. 'Mitch' added a DFC to his
decorations as well as the Italian Bronze
Medal for Military Valour. He died in 1974.

Tasmanian-born R.J. Brownell was with 45 Squadron in France prior to moving to Italy, having achieved five victories. In Italy he had brought his score to twelve by April 1918. He had won the Military Medal with the Australian Artillery during the Gallipoli campaign, and added the Military Cross while flying Camels. He retired from the RAF as an air commodore and died in 1974. On the last day of 1917 he shot down one Albatros and shared another 'kill'.

Camel B6238 was with 45 Squadron between August 1917 and February 1918. Henry Michael Moody from Shropshire claimed at least six victories in it, both in France and in Italy. Another 45 pilot, Earl Hand, shot down two Albatros Scouts on 11 January 1918 but these were disallowed by Wing and Brigade HQs. Hand, from Ontario, nevertheless scored four of his five victories in Italy.

Above left: Captain James Mitchell and Lieutenant Percy Wilson of 28 Squadron. Wilson, from Cheshire, joined the squadron in November 1917 and went on to become a flight commander in April 1918. Scoring a total of seven victories in Italy, he was rewarded with the Military Cross and the Italian Bronze Medal for Military Valour.

Above right: Captain Billy Barker DSO, MC with one of 28 Squadron's souvenir trophies.

Left: The Italian ace *Tenente* Silvio Scaroni, flying with the 76ª *Squadriglia*, who was involved in 28 Squadron's air fight on 26 December during which he claimed his ninth victory. He would go on to achieve twenty-six victories by July 1918, when he was wounded.

Chapter 2

Camels over the Piave

By January 1918 the battle-front in northern Italy had become firmly established along the Piave and Brenta rivers. As the armies on the Western Front had found, there was little movement to be had from offensives by from either side. However, in the air the British, Italian, French, Austrian and German airmen were able to penetrate across these rivers to engage in all the various forms of aerial activity, from reconnaissance and artillery observation to bombing and air fighting.

The Camel pilots of 45 Squadron started the year on New Year's Day with Second Lieutenant G.H. Bush claiming a Rumpler two-seater, while Captain Norman Macmillan sent down an Albatros Scout 'ooc' during an escort to a 34 Squadron RE8. However, 66 Squadron lost Captain Ralph Erskine (in B6414), shot down by *Leutnant* Ernst Fr. von Stenglin of Jasta 1. His CO Hans Kummetz also claimed a Camel inside allied lines but it was not confirmed. Erskine was from Glasgow and aged 25. Stenglin made six claims between January 1917 and January 1918 as a Leutnant, although only three may have been made official. He later became a bomber pilot with Bogohl III. Erskine had been leading an escort to 42 Squadron's RE8s bombing the German 14th Army HQ at Vittorio, along with 28 Squadron.

Over the next two days 45 Squadron added further victories, with Captain John Firth and Lieutenant H.T. Thompson flaming an Aviatik two-seater over Conegliano on the 2nd. On the 3rd Captain M.B. Frew and Second Lieutenant K.B. Montgomery shot down an Albatros D.III over Corbolone.

Matthew 'Bunty' Frew came from Glasgow and had served in France with the Highland Light Infantry before transferring to the RFC. Once trained as a pilot he was sent to 45 Squadron in April 1917 and by the time this unit converted to Camels in the summer, he and his observers had scored five victories on Sopwith two-seaters. By the end of 1917 he had achieved sixteen victories. It appears that the victory of 3 January went solely to Ken Montgomery. He too had been with 45 Squadron for some time, claiming four victories on Strutters, and this January claim was his eleventh. The Austrian pilot was probably Eugen Bönsch of Flik 51J, who force-landed his crippled machine. Bönsch was from Northern Bohemia (Czechoslovakia) of Sudeten-German parents and he was a victor in four combats by this date. He would go on to score sixteen. Montgomery hadn't put him out of the war, but no doubt he subsequently thought more about his mortality.

Barker of 28 Squadron had also opened the 1918 account by crashing an Albatros on the 1st but this, his eighth victory, was more certain for the German pilot from Jasta 1 was *Offizierstellvertreter (OStv,* Warrant Officer) Karl Lang, who did not survive the encounter. Barker had watched as the fighter hit the ground on a mountain, the burning wreckage rolling over and over down the mountainside.

On 6 January 45 Squadron lost the services of its veteran flight commander, Norman Macmillan MC, due to a stupid accident. Some pilots were fooling about around a bonfire and someone threw a petrol can across it but it fell into the flames and exploded, badly burning Macmillan and putting him out of the war. Fortunately he did not suffer permanent damage and in his later life remained closely associated with flying, receiving the Air Force Cross. He also wrote several books on flying, became a war correspondent and, upon retiring to Cornwall, became Deputy Lord Lieutenant of that county. He died in 1976.

The next successful combat came on the 10th, 45 Squadron claiming four enemy scouts, two destroyed and two 'ooc'. Second Lieutenants P. Carpenter and R.J. Brownell got the destroyed, Second Lieutenants D.W. Ross and T.F. Williams the 'oocs'. For Peter Carpenter from Cardiff it was his sixth victory, but his first on the Italian Front. He would become a high scorer with the squadron. Tom Williams from Ontario was something of a phenomenon. At this time he was 33 years old, positively ancient for a fighter pilot. He transferred from the Canadian Infantry in 1916 and joined 45 in France once he became a pilot. He was shot down twice before claiming his own first victory, once by the Red Baron (von Richthofen's) pilots and then by a Canadian machine-gunner as he and his flight commander (Firth) flew back over the lines at low altitude, the gunner mistaking them for Germans. This 10 January victory was his fifth and he would go on to almost triple this by July, at which time he was a flight commander with 28 Squadron.

If their four claims on the 10th were something to celebrate, eight on the 11th were even better. The claimants were Frew, Moody, Brownell, Williams, Firth, Earl Hand (2) and Thompson. All were D.IIIs with four destroyed and four 'ooc'. However, Wing HQ did not allow all of them. In this fight Jasta 1 lost its *Staffelführer, Oberleutnant* Hans Kummetz, over Conegliono. He was brought down by Lieutenant H.T. Thompson, who then found himself alone with four or five Albatros Scouts. He managed to evade their attentions, although his Camel was shot about and he himself suffered a slight wound. Short of fuel, he landed in a field without further problems and spent a few days in hospital. Henry Thompson, an Australian from New South Wales, later returned to his squadron. His Camel (B2494 'S') was rescued, repaired and flew again, only to be lost on 4 February after being hit by an artillery shell, killing Lieutenant D.G. McLean (see below).

Hans Kummetz had achieved seven victories with Jasta 1, six of them over France. His seventh had been Camel B4604 of 66 Squadron on 8 December 1917.

Vizefeldwebel Wilhelm Hippert of Jasta 39 shot down one of the Camel pilots, Second Lieutenant D.W.R. Ross, a Canadian, who was killed (B2436).

Second Lieutenant A.F. Lingard of 66 Squadron claimed the squadron's first 1918 victory on the 12th, another D.III destroyed south of Seren. On the 15th Bunty Frew claimed three victories, one DFW two-seater and a brace of Albatros Scouts. Peter Carpenter added a fourth with another V-strutter. Frew's total victories had now reached twenty. However, his Camel was hit by AA fire and although he landed safely, he suffered a neck injury. This did not correct itself and despite adding three more victories to his score, it forced him to stop combat flying. He returned to England to become an instructor. He received the DSO and Bar, MC and Bar and the Italian Silver Medal for Military Valour. He retired as Air Vice-Marshal Sir Matthew Frew, KBE and lived in South Africa until his death in May 1974. Peter Carpenter came from Cardiff, south Wales. This former milling student, once he had trained as a pilot, joined 45 Squadron in the summer of 1917 and by the time his unit was sent to Italy he had achieved five victories. He was another 45 pilot to score heavily, although he moved to 66 Squadron at the end of January as a flight commander, ending the war with twenty-four claims, a DSO, MC and Bar and the Italian Bronze Medal for Military Valour.

No. 66 Squadron lost its CO on 23 January. Major W.R. Gregory had a distinguished career with No. 40 Squadron during 1916–17, achieving eight victories and the Military Cross, and from the French the *Légion d'honneur* and *Croix de Guerre*. During a test flight it is thought that he fainted in the air and crashed to his death near Monastero. No. 66's new CO was Major J.M. Warnock until early February, at which time Major J.T.P. Whittaker took over.

Pilots of 28 Squadron encountered several two-seaters on the 25th, claiming three shot down. Lieutenant N.C. Jones claimed one and Lieutenant P. Wilson claimed one destroyed and one 'ooc'. These were Percy Wilson's first of eight victories. This Cheshire-born lad had joined the squadron in France after service with the Royal Engineers on the Western Front. Norman Jones, also from Cheshire, had joined the RFC from the artillery in Egypt in June 1917. This too was his first claim of a total of nine by late August, by which time he had become a flight commander with 45 Squadron.

On 27 January, *Unteroffizier* Amschl of Jasta 31 claimed a Camel shot down near Zenson for his first and only victory. However, no Camels were reported lost, so perhaps this was a misidentification.

February began with a loss to 66 Squadron with Lieutenant F.D.C. Gore flying B6207 (Australian) being shot down west of St. Vito by *Leutnant* Günther Keitsch of Jasta 39, and becoming a prisoner. Two days later, on the 4th, 45's Lieutenant D.G. McLean was flying escort to RE8s but ran into Albatros Scouts of Jasta 39.

Three German pilots each claimed a Camel, although McLean was the only loss; even so, it was thought that his Camel was hit by shellfire from an Italian battery! In the scrap, 45 claimed five Albatros D.IIIs shot down, one by Don McLean. This Canadian had only been with the squadron for thirteen days and had seen his victim go spinning down but then saw its pilot pull out, so McLean went for it again; this time it crashed, confirmed by other pilots and a British anti-aircraft gun battery. As McLean headed for home, so the Italian artillery shell struck his Camel (B2491 'S') and he was killed.

Captain H.B. Bell of 66 shot down two aircraft, one each on 4 and 6 February. These made it three in all for Hilliard Bell from Toronto. A former artillery man, he too would make flight commander, score ten victories and receive the Military Cross.

Other claimants on the 4th were from 45 Squadron, with the five Albatros Scouts shot down, Bunty Frew scoring twice. Meanwhile, 28 put in claims for three more Albatros Scouts. Jasta 39's three claims for Camels on the 4th were by *Oberleutnant* Josef Loeser, *Uffz.* Dierenfeld and *Leutnant* G. Schröder but with no Camels lost, these might have been Italian fighters, otherwise the Germans must have massively over-claimed. Even so, Loeser and Dierenfeld were both wounded, again reportedly by Camels. This combat is noted as taking place at 1130 hours and at 1300, the Jasta lost *Vizefeldwebel* Rudolf Wiesner in flames over Vittorio.

On the 5th, Barker and Hudson scored another three. Two were Scouts, while Barker's second was an Aviatik. The two had been sent to see off a two-seater directing artillery fire, escorted by two fighters, and eventually they spotted these three hostile aircraft and attacked. Barker attacked one piloted by *Zugsführer* Josef Schantl of Flik 19D, his gunfire causing a wing to rip away. Hudson engaged the other fighter, flown by *Fw (Feldwebel)* Karl Semelrock of Flik 51J, sending him down to crash. Barker, in the meantime, chased the two-seater, forcing it down in a spin. The enemy pilot recovered and in trying to land turned over, injuring both occupants.

Barker and Hudson were in evidence again on the 12th, out on a balloon hunt, although officially they were flying gun tests. There was thick ground mist above the Piave, giving them cover to sneak up on any balloons they saw up on the far side. In luck, they found five balloons at Fossamerlo: two large observation balloons and three small round ones hovering just above the ground (the purpose of the smaller ones is unclear). Both Camel pilots dived on their targets, sharing all five destroyed. There had been a sweepstake for the pilot who drew the name of the next pilot to down an enemy and upon their return, Barker walked into the mess and asked innocently if balloons counted in the sweep. He was told yes, to which he responded, 'Then whoever has drawn my name should get the money!' When asked why by Major Glanville, Barker replied, 'Because I've been out with Steve and we got two kite balloons and three comic gas bags.'

On the 20th, Lieutenant D.C. Wright of 28 Squadron was shot down and killed by *Leutnant* Wittenhagen of Jasta 31, while on 21 February 66 Squadron lost Second

Lieutenant A.B. Reade, shot down by ground fire during a ground strafing attack, flying B2514. The Camels had recently been fitted with bomb racks in order to carry four 20lb Cooper bombs for ground-attack sorties. The next day the squadron lost Captain Ken Montgomery (B4628), also brought down by ground fire. Wounded, he was taken prisoner and at the end of the war he was awarded the Italian Croce di Guerra. No. 28 Squadron also lost Second Lieutenant H. Butler in B6362 on the 22nd but he was killed.

Offizierstellvertreter Kurt Gruber of Flik 60J shot down one of 28 Squadron's pilots on the 25th, although he reported downing an Italian Hanriot. However, the British pilot survived the encounter with just a forced landing.

Captain Carpenter made his first claim with 66 Squadron on 27 February, an Albatros Scout destroyed. On the same day Lieutenant Alan Jerrard also made his first claim, a Berg fighter 'ooc'. The Berg D.I was usually referred to as the Berg Fighter in order to distinguish it from the parent Aviatik company in Germany, but it was designed locally for the Austro-Hungarian Air Service. It was not welcomed by pilots but continued to be engaged in combat throughout the war.

Jerrard, from Lewisham in London, had earlier been with the infantry prior to moving to the RFC. Initially assigned for two-seater training, his ability finally had him moved to fighters and an eventual posting to 19 Spad Squadron in France. His time there was short, as after being injured in a crash he was removed to hospital and once recovered was sent to 66 Squadron in Italy.

***

Major A.M. Vaucour, CO of 45 Squadron was, like all COs of the period, not required to fly combat so as not to risk the loss of such experienced pilots. However, 'Bunny' Vaucour had different ideas and tended to ignore these orders. On the 27th, he became an ace by downing two Albatros Scouts, adding them to his three claimed while flying Sopwith 1½ Strutters with 70 Squadron in France. Leaving the day-to-day patrols to his flight commanders, Vaucour often flew out alone, as on the 27th. Still on the west side of the Piave, he spotted three enemy scouts preparing to attack three Camels. So intent were the enemy pilots that they failed to spot Vaucour diving down on them until the leader, hit, broke away and dived to crash. Already Vaucour was firing at a second scout that also broke off and began to spin earthwards. The other Camels were from 28 Squadron and later they confirmed that one enemy scout had crashed with the other, seemingly 'ooc'. Famously, Vaucour's advice to new pilots was 'Never break formation, and should you ever find yourself alone in a fight, turn straight at the nearest enemy machine and fly for a collision…and never give way!'

Three stalwarts of 45 Squadron: Ken Montgomery MC, Bunty Frew DSO, MC and Peter Carpenter DSO, MC. Between them they would be credited with fifty-nine victories.

Captain Matthew Frew DSO, MC and Bar, from Scotland was credited with twenty-three victories by early February 1918; five over France, eighteen flying Camels over Italy. Suffering after a crash that forced his retirement from combat flying, he returned to England to become an instructor. He became Air Vice-Marshal Sir Matthew Frew, KBE, CB, DSO, MC, AFC and died in 1974.

Captain Kenneth Barbour Montgomery of 45 Squadron from Cheshire achieved four victories over France flying Sopwith 1½ Strutters, adding a further eight on Camels over Italy. He was awarded the Military Cross and sent to 66 Squadron as a flight commander. After attaining his twelfth victory on 12 January 1918, he was brought down by ground fire on 22 February, wounded and taken captive. Post-war he became a merchant in Liverpool.

Four 28 Squadron pilots: Lieutenants R.G.H. Davis, N.C. Jones, P. Wilson and G.H. McLeod. Percy Wilson was another Cheshire lad and he would achieve eight victories over Italy, be awarded the Military Cross and gain the Italian Bronze Medal for Military Valour. He became a flight commander in April 1918. Norman Jones, yet another Cheshire-born Camel pilot, born in Middlesbrough and later living in Altrincham, Cheshire, he achieved nine victories, one with 28 Squadron and eight with 45 Squadron on becoming a flight commander. He received the DFC. Jones came from a well-to-do family, having two servants, two nurses and a governess for him and his two sisters. He died in 1974. McLeod gained his first victory on 4 May 1918.

A photo of 28 Squadron's Norman Jones, on the left, with Lieutenant C.M. McEwen taken at Yatesbury prior to going to Italy. Clifford McEwen, from Manitoba, Canada, would end the war with twenty-seven victories and be awarded the MC, DFC and Bar, plus the Italian Bronze Medal. His nickname was 'Black Mike'. Post-war he joined the Royal Canadian Air Force, rising to Air Vice-Marshal. During the Second World War he commanded No. 6 (Canadian) Bomber Group in England and died in 1967.

Harold Byron Hudson, G.D. McLeod and Norman C. Jones of 28 Squadron. Hudson hailed from British Columbia, although he was born in Cobham, Surrey, his family having emigrated to Canada in 1912. With 28 Squadron he was in Billy Barker's flight and they often flew together. Known as 'Steve', he was awarded the MC and late in the war he was posted to 45 Squadron but all his thirteen victories were achieved with No. 28.

Captain T.F. Williams from Ontario joined the RFC in 1916, at the age of 30! With 45 Squadron he gained four victories over France, despite being shot down twice, once by a Canadian machine-gunner thinking he must be a German as he flew through a gun barrage over Passchendaele. For the first months of 1918 he continued to fly with 45 but was then made a flight commander with 28 Squadron, ending the war with thirteen victories and the Military Cross. He was known as 'Voss'.

Cedric Ernest Howell, known as 'Spike', came from Adelaide, Australia and saw action with the army in Egypt and Gallipoli prior to joining the RFC. Over Italy in 1918 with 45 Squadron he claimed nineteen combat victories and was awarded the DSO, MC and DFC. Surviving the war, he crashed and was drowned off Corfu in December 1919 while attempting to fly back to Australia in a Martinsyde A1 machine. The pilot on the right is Earl McNab Hand, a Canadian who claimed one victory over France and four more over Italy. Shot down in flames by the Austrian ace Frank Linke-Crawford on 1 June 1918, he survived, albeit badly burned, and was taken prisoner. Post-war he received the DFC and back in Canada he became a magistrate and helped form the Toronto Flying Club. He died in 1954.

Commanding 66 Squadron was Major W.R. Gregory MC, CdG (*Croix de Guerre*). He had earlier been with 40 Squadron in France, achieving eight victories flying FE8 and Nieuport Scouts. He was killed in a flying accident on 25 January 1918.

Captain Joe Mackereth of 28 Squadron from Essex, in front of Camel B6344, coded 'G'. Mackereth claimed six victories with the squadron and a seventh as a flight commander with 66 Squadron. Shooting down a kite balloon on 31 August 1918, he was hit by ground fire and wounded in the leg. He was forced to come down, whereupon he was taken prisoner.

Another shot of B6344 with its ground crew. Note the flight leader's pennant attached to the wing strut. Several 28 Squadron pilots flew in this particular Camel, including J.H. Mitchell, N.C. Jones, P.G. Mulholland, J. Mackereth, J.E. Hallonquist and Major O.M. Sutton.

Mechanics in front of a 28 Squadron Camel.

More mechanics by an A Flight Camel of 28 Squadron, coded 'A'.

Sopwith Camel B2376 of 45 Squadron, coded 'E'. Note the dumbbell squadron identity marking is not only on the fuselage side but also on the top decking. This machine was with the squadron between September 1917 and February 1918 and flown by K.B. Montgomery and R.J. Brownell.

Above left: Lieutenant Brian Davy, who flew with 28 Squadron in Italy in 1918.

Above right: Lieutenant Boyd H. Redner, also with 28 Squadron in 1918.

Right: Captain H.B. Bell MC, 66 Squadron. From Ontario, Hilliard Bell claimed ten victories over Italy and added the Italian Bronze Medal to his MC. Note the Aldis gun-sight. He signed himself as H. Brook Bell and died in 1960.

Best regards in appreciation of your work and thoughtfulness in Italy
W W McBain.

Second Lieutenant W.W. McBain, a Canadian, of C Flight, 28 Squadron, holding a wooden parrot mascot.

Above left: Three Canadians with 28 Squadron (top row): 'Black Mike' McEwen; Stan Stanger; Joe Hallonquist.

Above right: Four in less formal attire. Standing: McLeod and Joe Mackereth. Seated: Stan Stanger and Cliff McEwen.

Right: George Donald McLeod on the right, with two other unknown 28 Squadron personnel; the one with the ribbon of the MC has no flying badge, so can be assumed to be a staff officer.

McLeod's Camel pictured with its ground crew.

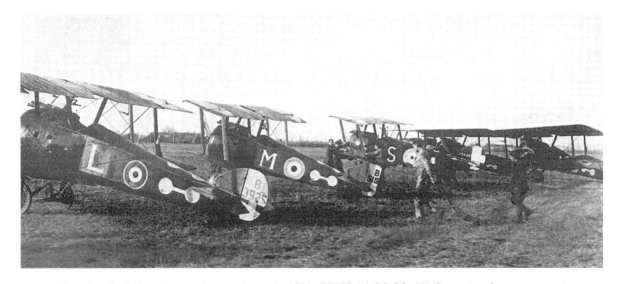

Camels of 45 Squadron at Istrana in early 1918. B3929 'L'; B5158 'M', flown by Carpenter and Montgomery; B2494 aircraft marked 'S' was flown by Lieutenant D.G. McLean on 2 February 1918 and he was killed when it received a direct hit from AA fire. Camel 'N' is B6354 flown by several pilots including John Firth, G.H. Bush, Jack Cottle, H.T. Thompson and Major Vaucour. Lieutenant G.C. Eaton was killed while flying the latter on 5 August 1918.

Major 'Bunny' Vaucour MC, CO of
45 Squadron from 24 August 1917.

Officers of 66 Squadron in the
spring of 1918. Standing: unknown;
W.H. Robinson (DoI 2 May); L.R. Willis;
C.M. Maud; F.S. Symondson; H.N.E. Row
(WIA 11 June);
R.G. Reid; unknown; H. Homan; Rudge;
unknown; G.F.M. Apps;
G.A. Birks; W.M. MacDonald.
Seated: J.S. Lennox; Captain J.M.
Warnock; Major J.T. Whittaker MC;
Captain H.B. Bell; Captain P. Carpenter
MC. On ground: N.S. Taylor; S. Stanger;
A. Jerrard; H.R. Eycott-Martin.

OffzSt. Kurt Gruber of Flik 60J. He claimed a Camel of 28 Squadron on 25 February, although the British pilot got away with just a forced landing. It was the Austrian's tenth victory. He was killed in action on 4 April 1918 in a fight with 66 Squadron's Camels. This picture was taken in 1916 while Gruber was flying with Flik 1 in Albatros B.1 two-seaters.

Camel B6344, 28 Squadron: flown by Mitchell in France, coded 'G', and in Italy was coded 1. Mitchell shot down Godwin Brumowski in this machine on 18 March 1918 and *Fw.* P.F. Hofstadter on 26 May. Joe Mackereth was brought down and captured in it on 29 October.

A 28 Squadron Camel, coded 'S', nosed over on landing. The squadron's identification mark was a white square.

Chapter 3

March – VC Action

Regarding successful air actions, March began slowly for the three Camel squadrons. On the 10th, 45's Second Lieutenants R.J. Dawes and J. Cottle shared in the destruction of a DFW C-type south-east of Salgereda. No. 66 Squadron lost Second Lieutenant W.G. Francis on a late afternoon patrol, last seen near Maserado. He was reported killed at Conegliano, flying B2377.

However, on the 11th 66 Squadron sent out a patrol led by Captain P. Carpenter and at 1140 hours they engaged a formation of Berg Scouts north of Valstagna. In the scrap that developed, Carpenter sent one down in flames, Lieutenant A. Jerrard crashed another and drove down a second, while Lieutenant G.F.M. Apps gained his first victory by sending down a Berg 'ooc'.

On the 18th, Captain Mitchell encountered an all-red Albatros D.V marked with a white skull, and sent it down on fire over Cordignano at 1530 hours. However, Mitchell was then shot up by two others flown by *Korporal* F. Schwarzmann and *Fw.* Stefan Fejes of Flik 51J, but he managed to get back across the lines. The pilot of the burning D.V also survived, its markings identifying Godwin Brumowski as the pilot. Brumowski of Flik 41J was a successful fighter pilot with a score of twenty-nine at this stage, and would go on to achieve thirty-five by mid-June.

Brumowski came from Wadowice, Galicia (now Poland), born into a military family. Graduating from the Military Academy in Mödling, near Vienna, in August 1910 he was commissioned into a field artillery regiment. When war came he saw action on the Russian Front, was decorated and then moved into aviation as an observer. After scoring two victories in this position, he then became a fighter pilot.

There was some change of bases at this time: 66 Squadron moved from Limbraga to Casa Piazza on the 10th, while on the 16th 45 Squadron began a transfer from Istrana to Grossa to join 28 Squadron. At the end of March, the RE8s of 34 Squadron moved from Istrana to Villaverla. Not far from Grossa, the Camels had to operate over some mountainous regions, rising in places to 12,000ft. The eastern end of their territory was the Brenta Valley, while to the west they covered an area to the Val d'Astico. Patrols were also flown up to the Tagliamento River from its Adriatic outfall, while to the west they could cover Feltre, Caldonazzo and Lake Garda. The area was very different from the Venetian plain of Istrana. In order to increase numbers of patrols, the Camel pilots began operating in threes rather than in sections of five.

Two of 66 Squadron's pilots, Stan Stanger and Francis Symondson, went off on a bombing expedition on the 14th and found two ships 5 miles off Miramara, near Trieste. They proceeded to drop their 20lb Cooper bombs on one of 200 tons and then worked it over with machine-gun fire, leaving it emitting smoke and flame.

The pilots of 66 Squadron continued their success in mid-month with claims of five enemy aircraft shot down between the 16th and the 19th. Then on the 21st in the hour after noon they claimed four more, including two for Peter Carpenter and one each for Alan Jerrard and Harold Eycott-Martin; the latter's first, a two-seater.

Major H.F. Glanville, CO of 28 Squadron, returned to England on the 19th, his place taken by Major C.A. Ridley DSO, MC. Claude Ridley, born in Sunderland, had already seen much active duty in France and against Zeppelins over England with home defence. Back in France he had flown into German-held territory to drop a spy but lost his engine and was forced down. He successfully evaded capture and escaped into neutral Holland. Some wondered why Barker had not been given command of 28, but he wasn't. Instead he was posted to 66 Squadron, in exchange for Captain J.M. Warnock who was meant to join 28. However, this New Zealander was showing signs of battle fatigue and never arrived, being posted back to England. Stan Stanger then took over a flight.

***

There was soon to be a change on the Italian Front as a result of the Germans' March offensive in France that began on the 20th. With a huge drive into the allied lines, British army units had to be withdrawn from Italy. They were relieved by Italian forces, while the few remaining British troops were redeployed onto a mountain plateau and the foothills of the Dolomites, defending approaches to the Lombardy Plain. The RFC's 14th Wing moved there as well.

In early March, the three German Jastas – 1, 31 and 39 – returned to the Western Front in anticipation of Germany's 'big push', known as Operation MICHAEL, which was planned to begin on the 20th. This left the Camels up against just Austro-Hungarian aircraft and pilots.

Gerald Birks and Gordon Apps each gained a further victory on 24 and 28 March. Birks came from Montreal and would achieve a dozen victories over Italy. Apps came from Kent and would also be a successful air fighter.

Meanwhile, 28 Squadron scored four victories on 18 and 19 March, with Billy Barker claiming three of them and Mitchell one, all Albatros Scouts. No. 45 Squadron also had an increase in air action in the latter part of the month with two claims on the 24th and three on the 27th, but only one was assumed as destroyed, an Albatros downed in flames by Second Lieutenant Tommy Williams, a D.III over Ceggia. Tommy was known as 'Voss'; this was his last victory while serving with

45 Squadron and was his eighth in total. He was soon moved to become a flight commander with 28 Squadron. At 32 years old, he showed little sign of his 'advanced age' compared to his younger companions.

***

Come 30 March 1918, 66 Squadron had recently moved its base from Treviso to San Pietro in Gu, north of Grossa. Bad weather prevented any flying till late morning, at which time three pilots were ordered to fly a patrol: Peter Carpenter, Eycott-Martin and Jerrard. Jerrard had slept late, so when he was called he put on his flying overall over his pyjamas!

Over the front at 1135 hours, the pilots spotted four Albatros Scouts escorting a two-seater and attacked. The actions of each side later became somewhat confused, the reports by the two surviving Camel pilots and the Austrians differing greatly. The two pilots to return were Carpenter and Eycott-Martin and their report remained unsigned by either man, but was approved and signed by the CO, Major J. Tudor Whittaker MC.

The report, which contains many anomalies, recorded that both Carpenter and Jerrard had destroyed an enemy fighter, and then Carpenter and Martin both observed Jerrard attacking other fighters. They were by now above an enemy airfield and Jerrard was said to be attacking enemy aircraft over the field as they attempted to take off. The two pilots reported some nineteen hostile aircraft in the air, six of which were being engaged by Jerrard. Martin went to his aid and claimed to shoot one off his companion's tail, while Jerrard shot down another. As the battle continued, Carpenter saw Jerrard shoot down an Albatros that had got onto Martin's tail, while Martin forced another to crash without firing a shot.

Jerrard was now surrounded by several Austrians and both Carpenter and Martin tried to help but were driven off by superior numbers, yet they saw Jerrard still fighting vigorously any enemy scout that came near him. He finally joined up with his two companions but appeared to be wounded. Ten Albatroses were following Jerrard who was lagging behind and Carpenter and Martin, being also closely engaged, were unable to go to his aid. They finally saw him, still attacking, but forced down to a crash-landing 4 miles west of Mansue aerodrome. He was taken prisoner.

In total, the three pilots appear to have downed six enemy fighters, three by Jerrard, two by Eycott-Martin and one by Carpenter. On the Austrian side, in part of their later report they quoted Jerrard's interrogation in which he claimed one Austrian shot down but then, with his engine beginning to misfire and run rough, he was chased by other fighters and shot down. There is no report by any Austrian unit of any attack upon their aerodromes.

Flik 32D was based at Mansue but the only fighter unit involved with Camels on this day was Flik 51J, based at Ghirano and commanded by *Oblt. (Oberleutnant)* Benno Fiala von Fernbrugg. His report gives a very different picture of events. Von Fernbrugg, with three other Albatros pilots, was returning from an escort sortie for a two-seater of Flik 32D and had just seen their charge land back at Mansue when they were attacked by three Camels. After an initial skirmish, von Fernbrugg fired into one Camel while another was engaged by *Offizierstellvertreter* Stefan Fejes. As von Fernbrugg headed south-west he saw the first Camel, Jerrard's, flying in the opposite direction.

The Austrian turned to the attack, firing 100 rounds into the Camel's engine and forward fuselage. Pulling up, he saw the Camel's nose drop and head for the front lines. He pursued and fired again and was joined by a companion, *Stabsfeldwebel* Eugen Bönsch, who also began firing at Jerrard's machine, but seeing his commander already in action, broke away. He then saw the Camel's propeller jerk to a halt, whereupon it made a crash-landing in a meadow north of Gorgo di Molino, some 2 miles south of Mansue. It hit a tree in doing so, ripping off both wings on the left side, then slithered to a stop and as the nose dug in, the tail section snapped off.

There was no fire and Jerrard was helped from the wreckage by nearby Austrian soldiers. Von Fernbrugg landed at Ghirano, about 4 kilometres from the scene, and quickly drove to the crash site, taking the still dazed Jerrard to the nearest army command post at Oderzo. Examining the wreckage, 163 bullet holes were counted, of which 27 had hit the petrol tank and 16 more were in the engine. Von Fernbrugg received credit for the kill, his fourteenth victory, although Fejes also put in a claim, though he had earlier been hit and suffered a slight wound to one foot.

The next day, Italian Command HQ recorded that six Austrian fighters had been shot down, later denied by Austrian Daily Summaries. Meanwhile, Whittaker's report had been forwarded to Wing HQ and the action was read with some enthusiasm by 'higher authority' and this resulted in Jerrard being awarded the Victoria Cross for his actions.

It has to be said that bearing in mind the Austrians did not report losing a single machine and only one pilot – who landed safely – suffered a slight foot wound, the claims were a trifle over-stated. The claim for six enemy fighters when the original hostile formation was only four aircraft was obviously enhanced by the inclusion of aircraft rising from the enemy airfield as Jerrard attacked. One has to wonder if HQ were waiting the arrival of a 'better than average' action report in order to publicize the RFC's actions over Italy, especially as British troops had recently started to be withdrawn from the front to help counter the German offensive in France. Whittaker's report, obviously rather colourfully written up, fitted the bill nicely. It certainly surprised Carpenter and Eycott-Martin and amazed poor Jerrard, now languishing in a prison camp in Salzburg.

What Jerrard recalled of the action was that while he encountered several enemy fighters and was near an Austrian airfield at times, the fight was very far from that supposedly reported by his two companions. When he finally decided to break off and head for the lines, he was very low and while no doubt hit by Fernbrugg's fire, the main damage was due to him hitting a tree as he hedge-hopped away and it was this that ripped off his port wings.

Returning home after the Armistice, Jerrard attended an investiture at Buckingham Palace on 5 April 1919. Remaining in the RAF post-war, he eventually retired due to poor health in 1933 with the rank of flight lieutenant. He died on 14 May 1968.

Carpenter received credit for one Albatros D.III destroyed, his thirteenth victory (of an eventual twenty-four), while Eycott-Martin was credited with two, his third and fourth of an eventual eight. When he later received the MC, the citation recorded his actions on 30 March. Carpenter had only recently received the MC, which presumably precluded any thought of another decoration, although he would end the war with the DSO, a Bar to his MC and the Italian Bronze Medal for Military Valour.

Jerrard's VC was the only one awarded to a Sopwith Camel pilot during the First World War, and the last to a Royal Flying Corps airman. The day after his action, 1 April 1918, the RFC became the Royal Air Force.

On the afternoon of the 30th, 66 Squadron was in action with other Austrian fighters near Mount Meletta. Lieutenant F.S. Symondson claimed one destroyed and Second Lieutenants H.N.E. Row and C. McEvoy reported one each 'ooc'.

***

The change from the RFC to the RAF made no difference to the fighting airmen, either in Italy or France. Nothing changed. However, it was 66 Squadron who scored first over Italy on 4 April; the same three 66 Squadron pilots who scored on the afternoon of the 30th, three Albatros Scouts destroyed, one in flames over Cismon: Symondson, Row and McEvoy. One of the opposing pilots was Kurt Gruber of Flik 60J. The Austrian had a score of ten Italian aircraft and balloons, some scored on the Russian front. On the 4th his Phönix D.I fighter began to disintegrate in the fight with 66 Squadron and he fell to his death.

Second Lieutenant H.B. Holman died in an accident on the 4th flying B5226, having choked his engine just after becoming airborne.

Then air actions became scarce until the 17th, once again 66 Squadron being to the fore with Carpenter scoring over a D.V at 0950 hours, and then Barker downed another Albatros south of Vittorio at 1100. In mid-afternoon Symondson got two more and Row and McEvoy one apiece, making a total of six for the day.

Captain R.J. Brownell of 45 Squadron claimed a D.III 'ooc' on the same day, while 28 bagged four, one each to Messrs Mitchell, A.F. White, G.W. McLeod and

J.E. Hallonquist. Brownell scored again on the following day, but the next victory claims did not come until the 23rd, Second Lieutenants E. McNab Hand and C.E. Howell of 45 destroying two D.IIIs north of Levico.

That was it for April. There had been some losses. During the fighting on the 17th 28 Squadron lost Lieutenant W.G. Hargreave killed in combat (B6342) and on the 23rd Captain C.J. Thomson-Curweth was brought down by ground fire and taken prisoner (B5401). Hargreave was claimed following the attentions of two Austrian pilots, Godwin Brumowski and Friedrich Navratil from Flik 41J. This was Brumowski's thirty-first victory but Navratil's first of an eventual ten. However, Stefan Fejes of Flik 51J also claimed a Camel on the 17th.

Another event on 17 April was that Barker left 28 Squadron to become a flight commander with 66 Squadron. By this time his personal victory score was twenty-three, all scored in Camel B6313. Unusually, he was allowed to take this machine along with him to 66 Squadron. He had been awarded the DSO, MC and Bar, with a second Bar gazetted on 24 April.

Hauptmann Godwin Brumowski, CO of Flik 41J, standing by his Albatros Scout which carried his personal marking of a white skull. On 18 March 1918 he was lucky to survive an encounter with John Mitchell of 28 Squadron.

Above left: A more formal picture of Brumowski, duly autographed, and with the monocle of a gentleman. Brumowski was 28 years old at this time and he survived the war with thirty-five victories. His decorations include the Order of the Iron Cross, Knight's Cross of the Order of Leopold and the Gold Bravery Award to Officers. In 1930 he opened a flying school near Vienna but died in a crash at Schiphol Airport, Amsterdam in June 1936.

Above right Captain Peter Carpenter MC, who led Harry Eycott-Martin and Alan Jerrard on the fateful patrol on 30 March 1918, leading to an air battle with Albatros fighters of Flik 51J.

Opposite above: The skull-marked Albatros of Godwin Brumowski showing the fire damage to the top centre section and the inner section of the lower starboard wing. For Brumowski it had to be a terrifying experience as the flames of the burning canvas roared back over his head as he desperately tried to get his machine down to what appears to have been a good landing.

Opposite below: Another Brumowski crash-landing following a combat in April 1918, during which his lower wings broke. Again, he was lucky to survive.

Above left: Lieutenant H.R. Eycott-Martin of 66 Squadron. Born in Norwood, he was living in Lindfield, Sussex when war came and after serving with the Royal Engineers as a signaller, he transferred to the RFC. Injured in a crash with 41 Squadron, upon recovery he was posted to 66 in Italy during February 1918. He was credited with two victories on 30 March.

Above right: Second Lieutenant Alan Jerrard of 66 Squadron initially served with the 5th South Staffordshire Regiment, moving to the RFC in 1915. Flying Spads with 19 Squadron, he did not get off to a good start by becoming lost and crashing his machine. Like Eycott-Martin, he too found himself posted to Italy after recovering from his injuries. By 30 March 1918 he had achieved four victories but was shot down on this date. While a prisoner of the Austrians he learned that he had been awarded the Victoria Cross, due to the report made by his squadron commander.

Opposite above: The wreck of Alan Jerrard's Sopwith Camel (B5648). The left-hand planes had been ripped off in the crash-landing and as the machine snapped forward onto its nose, the tail-plane broke off.

Opposite below: A dejected Alan Jerrard by the wreckage of his Camel shortly after being pulled from the debris by Austrian soldiers.

Alan Jerrard remained in the RAF post-war until released due to ill health in 1933. This picture is of him as a flight lieutenant during the 1930s with his VC ribbon. The Italians also awarded him their Bronze Medal for Military Valour (*Medaglia di Bronzo al Valore Militare*). He died in May 1968.

Oberleutnant Benno Fiala von Fernbrugg of Flik 51J who shot down Alan Jerrard on 30 March 1918. He would survive the war with twenty-eight victories. A native of Vienna and a former artillery officer, he had followed his brother into aviation pre-war, Otto having been a naval flyer. He remained closely associated with flying post-war and served in the *Luftwaffe* in the Second World War. He died in October 1964.

A few pilots of Flik 51J. L to R: Stefan Fejes (sixteen victories); Michael Dorcie; Fiala von Fernbrugg; Franz Rudorfer (eleven victories); Eugene Bönsch (sixteen victories). Fejes and Bönsch had been involved in the action of 30 March.

Captain J.H. Mitchell MC, pictured later in the war with the first design DFC ribbon next to the MC. He gained his ninth victory on 17 April 1918. He too would receive the Italian Bronze Medal for Military Valour. He died in 1974.

Lieutenant Gordon F.M. Apps of
66 Squadron gained his first two
victories in March 1918, bringing his
score to ten by mid-July when he was
wounded and was awarded the DFC.
Post-war he served with the RCAF but
was killed in a flying accident in 1931.

Lieutenant S. Waltho, one of 28 Squadron's original pilots. He claimed his first and only victory on 27 February 1918.

Lieutenant F.S. Symondson, 66 Squadron. Francis Symondson came from Sutton, Surrey but later lived in Bromley. On 7 March he burned a balloon and shot down two enemy aircraft before the end of that month. He ended the war with eleven victories, the MC and Italian Bronze Medal. Post-war he remained closely associated with flying and died in 1975.

Lieutenant Christopher McEvoy from North London gained his first victory with 66 Squadron on 30 March 1918 and went on to achieve a total of nine victories. Receiving the DFC later in the year, he returned to England to fly on home defence duties. In the Second World War he was a cipher officer with Coastal Command. He died in 1952. His younger brother was Air Chief Marshal Sir Theodore McEvoy, KCB, CBE.

Tasmanian-born Captain R.J. Brownell, following service with the army at Gallipoli, flew with 45 Squadron, achieving his last two victories in April 1918. He had served in both France and Italy and received the MC for his twelve victories. He retired from the RAF as an air commodore CBE but died in 1974 in Perth, Western Australia. He had received the Military Medal for his earlier army service.

Above: Sopwith Camel B6285 'C' of 28 Squadron was with this unit from September 1917 until being 'Struck off Charge' in March 1918. It was often flown by Lieutenant A.G. Jarvis. Note the streamer attached to the rudder, denoting a deputy flight leader.

Opposite above: Some of 45 Squadron at Grossa. L to R: J.E. Child; C.E. Howell; J.P. Huins; H.D. O'Neill; T.F. Williams; H.M. Moody; G.H. Bush; C.G. Catto. James (Jack) Escott Child came from Surrey and achieved five victories in France and Italy; he died on 3 November 1918, probably in the influenza pandemic. Cedric Ernest Howell, known as 'Spike', was born in Adelaide and served at Gallipoli before moving to aviation; awarded the DSO, MC and DFC, he had nineteen victories; died in a crash flying back to Australia in December 1919. James Proctor 'Proc' Huins gained three victories; after the war he became an RAF doctor LRCP MRCS, receiving not only the Air Force Cross and Bar, but made an OBE before going into private practice in Dursley, Glos. H.D. 'Paddy' O'Neill gained three victories. Thomas Frederic Williams from Ontario had fourteen victories, was awarded the MC and DFC; he died just two months short of his 100th birthday in July 1985. Henry Michael Moody from Shropshire gained eight victories and was awarded the MC; he remained in the RAF but was killed in a collision in the air in April 1931. G.H. Bush, an Australian and post-war a lawyer, gained three victories. Charles Gray Catto from Dallas, Texas gained six victories over Italy; he became a doctor after the war.

Opposite below: The Camels of 45 Squadron had a white dumbbell as their identification marking. B6372 'H' was often flown by Captain M.B. 'Bunty' Frew, seen here in the snow during the winter of 1917 together with his ground crew.

Camel B5401 'E', showing clearly the 28 Squadron marking of a white square on the fuselage side. Note also the difference in serial number type and placement, and a flight leader pennant on the elevator (there would also be one on the other side). Captain C.J. Thomson-Curweth was shot down by ground fire in this machine on 23 April 1918 to be taken prisoner. The 'E' and the white square are repeated on the top wing centre section.

Major J.T. Whittaker MC, commanding officer of 66 Squadron in Italy. It was his report following an interview with Peter Carpenter and Harold Eycott-Martin on Jerrard's actions on 30 March 1918 that led to the latter's award of the Victoria Cross. For his service in Italy he received the Italian *Croce al Merito di Guerre*, the Order of the Crown of Italy (*Ordine della Corona d'Italia*) and the *Medaglia d'Argento al Valore Militare* (Silver). He remained in the RAF post-war but died in India in 1927 commanding 28 Squadron.

What well-dressed pilots were wearing in 1918: shorts and fug boots. This is Lieutenant Harry King Goode while with 66 Squadron. He would be awarded the DSO and DFC in Italy and claim a total of fifteen victories.

Chapter 4

Before the Battle of the Piave

The poor April weather had curtailed much operational flying, but in May it picked up. During May the three Camel squadrons would claim over eighty enemy aircraft shot down. Most operations were now over the Asiago front and the Camel squadrons began to fly two-man patrols.

Among the claimants in 45 Squadron were Lieutenants Earl McNab Hand, Cedric Howell, Ernest H. Masters, Jack Cottle, Charles Catto and Captains Norman C. Jones and George H. Bush. Masters, from Coventry, was only 19 years old but opened his account on 13 May with an Albatros and an LVG destroyed. He would go on to claim eight victories and be awarded the *Croix de Guerre*, only to die in an aerial collision on Christmas Eve 1918.

Jack Cottle came from Plymouth in Devon, but had spent his early years in Zululand. He joined the South African Mounted Rifles in 1914 before moving into aviation. His first victory with 45 had been over a DFW on 10 March; his second an Albatros D.III in flames on 18 May. He would go on to score eleven victories over Italy, adding two more when 45 returned to France in late 1918. He received the DFC.

George Bush, from Australia, claimed four victories with the squadron, including a Berg D.I that he and Voss Williams brought down inside allied lines on 2 February. His last victory came on 22 May, an LVG. The Berg fighter was the first taken virtually intact by the allies, its pilot being a Hungarian, *Korporal* Andras Kilczar, who was captured and despite his lowly rank, was taken to the 45's officers' mess for a drink. After the war Bush became a lawyer.

The scorers during May in 28 Squadron consisted of Stan Stanger, Christopher McEwen, Percy Wilson, R.J. 'Dickie' Dawes, John Mackereth, Arthur Cooper, Harold Hudson, P.G. Mulholland, O.W. Frayne, G.D. McLeod, Mitchell and Joe Hallonquist. In all, there were around twenty-six claims.

One with interesting post-war revelations was that on 2 May, Stanger and Hudson were out on patrol and spotted an Austrian two-seater with a close escort of three Albatros Scouts, while some way higher and behind were six more Scouts. As the two Camel pilots approached, they saw the four machines start to turn away, but then the Scouts headed down. So too did the upper six, leaving the poor two-seater totally alone. Stanger took the opportunity, closed in and after a good long burst, the two-seater went down in flames. It later transpired that the Scouts were from Flik 51J commanded by Brumowski, and there had been an enquiry into how they had all abandoned the recce machine. Flik 51J were exonerated, however, when they said they had been approached by a 'large force' of Camels.

On 4 May, 45 Squadron was ordered to bomb the Trentino hydro-electric power station which was situated in an awkward valley north of Lake Garda. George Bush led Messrs Ernest Child, Spike Howell, Jack Cottle, James Black and Lingard, leaving at 0930 hours. Due to the difficult approach, no bombs hit the target until Howell, being last to go in and seeing how difficult the others had found it, approached from another angle and saw his four bombs falling into the target area, two bursting on the station while another hit a large building.

The squadron intended to try again on the 13th, with Howell leading Masters and Bowles. Taking off at 0510, they ran into ten enemy aircraft on the way. With the advantage of an early low sun behind them, the three Camel pilots waded in and claimed five shot down: three plus one out of control by Howell, and a D.III by Masters, who also shared an LVG two-seater with Bowles.

John Mackereth's May contribution was a balloon on the 19th. From Essex, Mac reported making no fewer than six attacks on the balloon before it finally erupted in flames. It was his first of seven victories. Arthur Gabbettis Cooper was another Essex lad and served with 28 from 8 October 1917 until 2 July 1918, during which time he downed seven enemy machines, including three on 19 May: two Albatros D.Vs destroyed plus one 'ooc'. He received the Italian *Croce di Guerra*. Cooper was killed in a flying accident at Weymouth in 1928, flying his personal Avro 504K.

Stan Stanger came from Montreal, Canada, joining the RFC after some thirty months in the 56th Westmount Rifles, 4th Canadian Ammunition Supply Park, attached to the 1st Canadian Artillery Regiment. He joined 66 Squadron shortly before the move to Italy but at the end of April 1918 became a flight commander with 28 Squadron. For his thirteen victories he received the MC and DFC. One day in October 1918, Stanger became ill in the air, felt disorientated and, seeing an airfield below, he went down and landed, only to discover it was in Austrian hands. He had switched off his engine but before the Austrians realized what was happening, Stanger took off his flying boots and using them as wheel chocks, swung the propeller, got his engine going and took off again. He died in his home town in 1967.

Richard Jeffries 'Dickie' Dawes came from Lachine, Quebec. His one victory with 28 Squadron came on 3 May. He had earlier been with 45 Squadron in France and Italy, and returned to this unit as a flight commander. By mid-June he had achieved nine victories. On returning to the UK, he received the DFC. He returned to Canada and died in 1983.

Wilson came from Cheshire, and had been with 28 since November 1917. He became a flight commander in April 1918 and his four victories in May brought his score to eight. He received the MC and the Italian Bronze Medal. Meanwhile Harold Hudson scored his last three victories during May, bringing his score to thirteen. 'Steve' Hudson had emigrated to Canada from Surrey with his family in 1912, aged 14. He was awarded the MC, and post-war was employed in the paper mill industry. He died in Vancouver in 1981.

Joseph Eskel Hallonquist was born in Mission City, British Columbia and before joining the army had been a bank clerk. Following service with the 128th and 210th battalions of the Canadian Expeditionary Force, he had moved to aviation and found himself posted to Italy and 28 Squadron at the beginning of 1918. He made captain and was awarded both the DFC and Italian Bronze Medal for his five victories. He was shot down on 29 October but survived the final days of the First World War as a prisoner. Returning to Canada, he became an insurance salesman but died of a heart attack in 1958.

No. 28 Squadron lost a pilot on the morning of 11 May: Lieutenant E.G. Forder in Camel B2455 'X'. Captain Wilson led an escort mission that was attacked by some Albatros Scouts. Wilson and Lieutenant O.W. Frayne each claimed one shot down but Forder was lost, shot down by Frank Linke-Crawford, leader of Flik 60J. Linke-Crawford had been born in Cracow, Poland, the son of an army major who had married an English lady, Lucy Crawford. After serving with the army and cavalry on the Eastern Front, he moved to aviation and became an observer, later training as a pilot flying two-seater bombing and reconnaissance missions. He survived a shoot-down on 2 August 1917, his victor thought to have been the Italian ace Pier Ruggero Piccio (twenty-four victories in the First World War). Forder managed a forced landing to become a prisoner. He was Linke-Crawford's twenty-third victory.

During May, 66 Squadron put in claims for almost fifty enemy machines shot down, many deemed to be destroyed. Among the claimants was Barker, of course, with eight, bringing his score to thirty-one. The other flight commanders at this stage were C.M. Maud and H.B. Bell. Charles Maud was a Yorkshireman from near Leeds, who had transferred to the RFC from the Royal Field Artillery. He was still only 21 years old when he joined 66 in Italy. His first five victories were all scored in May, and his final total reached eleven by the war's end. He too received the DFC, and he died in 1974.

Hilliard Brooke Bell from Toronto was another former artilleryman. He joined 66 shortly before the move to Italy and scored his seventh and eighth victories in May 1918, adding two more in July. He received the MC and the Italian Bronze Medal before returning to England. Post-war he became a lawyer and a distinguished career was topped when he was appointed as King's Counsel. He died in his home town in 1960.

There were multiple claims in early May for 66: two on the 1st, four on the 2nd, five on the 3rd, six on the 4th and three on the 6th. H.K. Boyson, G.F.M. Apps, G.A. Birks, F.S. Symondson and W.C. Hilborn all scored. Howard Koch Boyson, an American from Illinois, had been a trainee mining engineer and joined the RFC in Canada. He joined 66 Squadron in France, made ace during May 1918 and received the Italian Silver Medal. Back in the UK he flew with home defence squadrons until he returned home in 1919. He was living in Houston, Texas when he died in 1963.

Gordon Apps became an ace in May, and before he was wounded on 16 July had scored ten victories. He received the DFC. After the war he lived in Canada, joining the RCAF, but was killed in a flying accident in 1931.

Gerald Alfred Birks from Montreal scored no fewer than eight victories in May, bringing his score to ten, to which he added two more in June. Two kills on 4 May were brought down inside Italian lines, both Albatros Scouts at Vidor. They were from Flik 61J and both pilots, *Leutnants* F. Frisch and K. Patzelt, were killed. Karl Patzelt began his military flying as an observer, learning to fly while under unofficial training by his pilots. In his observer role he scored two victories over Italian Nieuport Scouts, and then in November 1917 as a pilot with Flik 42J he brought his score to five. In February 1918 he was given command of Flik 68J. Birks received the MC and Bar, returning home to join the family jewellery business before becoming an investment banker. He died in 1991. (We shall read more of Birks later in this chapter.)

Francis Stanley Symondson, born in Sutton, Surrey, was living in Bromley, Kent when he joined the RFC. Posted to 29 Squadron in France, he crashed three Nieuports and was sent home for further training. This must have done him some good, for returning to operations with 66 Squadron in Italy he achieved thirteen victories during 1918, including two on 6 May. He received the MC and the Italian Silver Medal, ending the war as a captain. He continued to fly post-war, mostly in light sport aircraft. He served in the Second World War as a code and cipher officer, dying in 1975.

William Carroll Hilborn from British Columbia had the experience of flying with all three Camel squadrons in Italy. He joined 66 Squadron in November 1917 but did not bring down his first enemy aircraft till 1 May 1918, raising his score to four by the end of the month. He then went to 28 Squadron where he gained his seventh and final kill on 12 August. The next day he became a flight commander with 45 Squadron, but was fatally injured in a crash on the 16th. His award of the DFC was gazetted in November.

***

More fights and claims during May 1918 were, in some ways, topped on the 24th with the loss of one of the Austro-Hungarians' leading aces at the time. Josef (József) Kiss was 22 years of age, the son of a gardener, but upon leaving school to enlist in the army, his lack of qualifications did not allow for a commission. He was sent to the Russian front as an infantry soldier where he was wounded. Upon recovery he decided to join the flying service and by late 1916 was flying reconnaissance machines over the Southern Tyrol. His first three victories were shared with his observers but he was then allowed to fly a single-seater Berg D.I on protection sorties. With a score of seven he was shot down on 17 September but survived.

Becoming a fighter pilot in November, he joined Flik 55J, where he often accompanied another ace, Julius Arigi. By late January 1918, Kiss had a victory tally of nineteen and had won four silver and three gold bravery medals. However, on 27 January he was badly wounded in action. Returning to active duty, probably too soon, he was engaged in a fight with 66 Squadron on 24 May near Lamon at 1100 hours.

Kiss was based at Pergine, flying Phönix D.IIa fighters, Kiss in 422.10. Nearby was Flik 60J, based at Feltre, under the command of *Oblt.* Frank Linke-Crawford (twenty-three victories by this date). Both units were alerted to the approach of Italian Caproni bombers. Kiss and two companions took off and joined up with aircraft from Flik 60J, but before sighting the bombers, they spotted Sopwith Camels. Billy Barker had flown out with Apps and Birks and it was these that the Austrians had sighted. In the fight that followed, Barker sent one down in a spin, while Birks attacked another, whose wings crumpled and tore away.

Both sides over-claimed, as with the Jerrard fight back in March. No. 66 Squadron reported four enemy machines shot down, while the Austrians said two Camels had crashed. In the event, no Camels were lost and only one Austrian fighter crashed. The pilot of this machine was so badly crushed that he could only be recognized by his medal ribbons. It was Kiss. Whether it was Barker or Birks that fired the fatal shots is not really known, but it is generally believed it was Gerry Birks. Kiss had been the most successful Hungarian-born ace.

A sad postscript to Kiss's life was that he had a girlfriend by the name of Enrica Bonecker living near the airfield at Pergine. She never married and it is said that she visited his grave every day for the next fifty-two years of her life. In 1970, Kiss's remains were removed to a large war memorial ossuary at Rovereto, Italy. Discovered among the bones was Kiss's watch, which had stopped at 11.00 am, the time of the air fight.

On 26 May, Captain Mitchell downed his tenth hostile aircraft, identified as being *Fw.* P.F. Hofstadler of Flik 42J (153:230). Jim Mitchell would score one more victory in early June, and then returned to England in the following month. He died in 1974. Also on the 26th, Joe Hallonquist claimed an Albatros D.V east of Fontanelle. The enemy pilot was *Zgsf.* Ferdinand Udvardy of Flik 42J, who managed a crash-landing.

Udvardy ended the war with the rank of *Stabsfeldwebel* with a total of eight victories, having been awarded the Gold Bravery Medal twice and the Silver Bravery Medal, 1st Class, three times. He was born in Pozsony, Czechoslovakia, of Hungarian parents and had been a soldier before becoming a pilot. In 1919, flying against the Romanians with the Red Air Force, he downed another hostile aircraft.

On the 30th, thirty-five Camels from all three fighter squadrons made a massed attack at Val d'Assa, dropping bombs and expending 9,000 rounds of ammunition. Along with them flew Major Ridley, Stanger and Mackereth as unofficial escort and observers. This was in support of an offensive in this area. At least twenty-eight bombs hits were seen on building, trucks and wagons, and the Camel pilots expended some 9,135 rounds of .303 ammunition into scattering ground troops. Jack Cottle was the only casualty, being hit and wounded by ground fire while flying B7360 'N'. Howard Boyson (B5180) destroyed an Albatros, flown by *Offizierstellvertreter* Karl Gebhard of Flik 41J, for his fifth and final victory.

Lieutenant Charles G. Catto, an American who flew with 45 Squadron in Italy. Dallas-born, he was a medical student at Edinburgh University in 1914. Once his studies had been completed, he joined the British army and then moved to the RFC in June 1917. He achieved six victories and after the war became a doctor. This picture was taken following the completion of his flying tests, thereby gaining his Royal Aero Club flying certificate. He died in 1972.

Austrian Brandenburg C.I two-seater shot down by Catto on 7 June, a machine of Flik 8D.

Some of 45 Squadron taking a break from operations. L to R: unknown; G. McIntyre; J.R. Black; F.S. Bowles; C.G. Catto; E H. Masters. Black and Bowles both scored one or two victories, while Ernest Masters achieved eight to receive the French *Croix de Guerre*. He was killed in an aerial collision on 24 December 1918, aged just 19.

Four of 45 Squadron on leave in Venice: Charles Catto; unknown; J.C.B. Firth MC; H.B. Hudson.

Above: Camel B3840 'F' of 66 Squadron, tipped up on its nose. Lieutenant W.H. Robinson was killed in this aircraft in a crash on 2 May 1918.

Left: *Oberleutnant* Karl Patzelt, CO of Flik 68J. With other units he had claimed five victories in 1917, but on 4 May 1918 he was shot down by Gerald Birks of 66 Squadron and killed.

Opposite above: Captain Barker standing by his twenty-eighth victory, a Lloyd two-seater shot down inside Italian lines on 21 May 1918 at Colmello. Its pilot had been on a lone reconnaissance mission, without an observer. The pilot gave up the struggle and attempted a landing, but as he touched down his machine turned over as it ripped off its wheels.

Opposite below: Some of the pilots of 28 Squadron pose for the camera. L to R: unknown; Joe Mackereth; unknown; Peter Wilson; Gordon F.M. Apps (66 Squadron); Harold B. Hudson; unknown; Stan Stanger; unknown; Stanton, Waltho; unknown.

Captains James Mitchell MC, DFC and Percy Wilson MC of 28 Squadron.

Captain Percy Wilson standing by some of 28 Squadron's war trophies.

Captain Stanley Stanger MC, DFC from Montreal. A thirteen-victory ace, he flew Camels with both 66 and 28 Squadrons in Italy. Post-war he worked in the family business, the Guardian Trust Co. of Montreal, becoming president in 1939. He remained so until shortly before his death in 1967.

A smiling Joe Hallonquist, second from left, front row. The picture was taken at Grossa with other members of B Flight, 28 Squadron. He scored five official victories and at least one more unconfirmed. On 26 May 1918 he shot down Ferdinand Udvardy of Flik 42J.

Ferdinand Udvardy of Flik 42J, forced into a crash-landing by Joe Hallonquist on 26 May.

Sopwith Camel B2455 'X' of 66 Squadron, in which Lieutenant E.G. Forder was forced down by *Oberleutnant* Frank Linke-Crawford of Flik 60J on 11 May 1918. Having landed virtually intact, it was repainted with Austrian markings and test-flown by Austrian pilots. Forder became a prisoner.

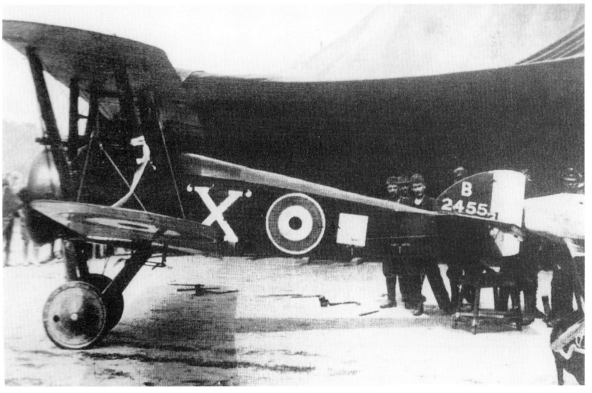

Oberleutnant Frank Linke-Crawford. Polish-born, he served in cavalry units on the Eastern Front before moving to aviation. At first he flew as an observer but on becoming a pilot he gained thirteen victories between August and December 1917 with Flik 41J, and then went to Flik 60J as its commander. Forder was his twenty-third victory. Linke-Crawford is standing in front of his Albatros D.III with its falcon insignia

Gerald Birks was awarded the MC and Bar for his work with 66 Squadron. Born in Montreal, Canada, he achieved twelve official combat victories in the first half of 1918 before being rested.

Sopwith Camel D8101 'P' of 66 Squadron. Gerry Birks claimed his last two victories in this machine in June 1918 and fellow Canadian William Hilborn shot down his fifth victory in it on 18 July. Other pilots to score while flying this Camel were Gordon Apps (18 July); Lieutenant A.E. Baker (20 July); Lieutenant H. deC. McDiarmid (15 August). After a refit it was sent to 28 Squadron. In this picture the engine cowling has been removed to let mechanics work on the rotary engine.

William Carroll Hilborn from Alexandria, British Columbia. Between May and August 1918 he claimed six victories and was awarded the DFC. His final victory was claimed following his appointment as a flight commander with 28 Squadron. He was badly injured in a flying accident on 13 August and died on the 26th.

Left: Gerry Birks and Stan Stanger of 66 Squadron. Note the thick sheepskin flying boots.

Right: An American from Dallas, Texas, Howard Koch Boyson joined the RFC in Canada. He joined 66 Squadron in France while still flying Sopwith Pups and it was not until early December that he downed his first enemy aircraft, but while flying a Camel. In total he claimed five victories and received the Italian Silver Medal for Military Valour.

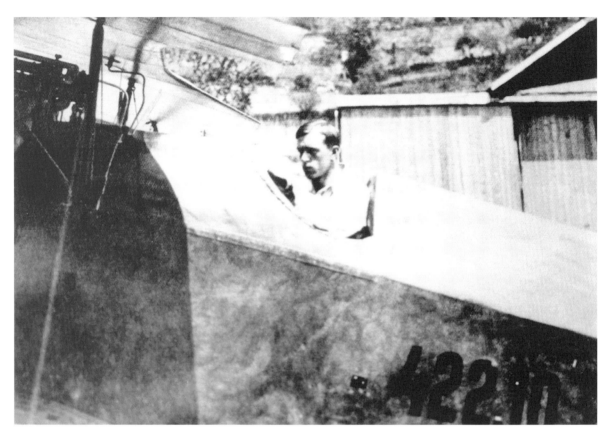

Josef 'Josi' Kiss of Flik 55J. His humble beginnings meant that he remained an NCO pilot with the Austrians; nevertheless, flying both two-seaters and later single-seater fighters, he achieved nineteen victories before being badly wounded on 27 January 1918. By May he felt ready to return to operations, although he was advised against it. Flying on 24 May he was shot down and killed in a fight with Camels of 66 Squadron, either by Gerry Birks or Will Barker. He was posthumously made a *Leutnant*. He is pictured here in a Phönix D.II fighter (422.10), the machine in which he died.

Josef Kiss in front of a large Caproni bombing aeroplane. Note the double-banked wheels and a skid.

Captain W.G. 'Billy' Barker standing by his famous Camel, B6313. Discernible on the right-hand gun is the flat metal shape of a red devil, thumbing its nose to any enemy that had the bad luck to find itself in front of Barker's machine.

Oberleutnant Friedrich Navratil. Flying with Flik 41J, his first victory was the Camel flown by Lieutenant W.G. Hargreaves of 28 Squadron (B6342). He went on to achieve ten victories, including two BF2b machines of 139 Squadron, one in July, the other in August 1918, flying with Flik 3J. Surviving the First World War, in the second he was a general with the Yugoslav Air Force and later Minister of Defence in Croatia. As the war ended, he was tried by a 'people's court' by the Tito government for war crimes and sentenced to death in 1946.

Frank Linke-Crawford in serious mood, thumbs in pockets, as he tries to ignore the photographer.

The two pilots are Godwin Brumowski and Frank Linke-Crawford, in front of two Albatros D.III fighters, probably numbered 153.52 and 153.16. Both men flew with Flik 41J in late 1917. Note the left-hand machine has Brumowski's white skull marking on the fuselage, while Linke-Crawford has a large spread-wing falcon on his. Like von Richthofen on the Western Front, Brumowski's machine was bright red, the skull being repeated on the top fuselage decking.

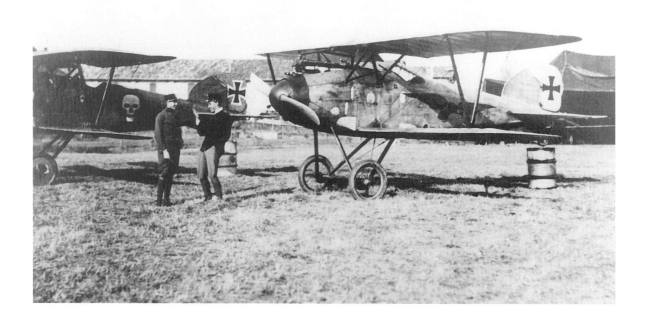

Sopwith Camel B6354 'N' of 45 Squadron. Several successful pilots flew this machine in combat including J.C.B. Firth, G.H. Bush, Jack Cottle and J.P. Huins. It was lost on 5 August 1918, with Lieutenant G.C. Easton being killed.

Camel 'P' of 66 Squadron, flown by Gerald Birks MC. Birks, a Canadian from Montreal, achieved twelve victories between March and June 1918 and was awarded the MC and Bar.

Lieutenant Harold Byron Hudson from Victoria, British Columbia; born in Cobham, Surrey. Known as 'Steve', he often flew with his flight commander, Will Barker, and was awarded the MC. Among his score of thirteen victories were seven balloons, all shared with Barker. Before leaving Italy, he served briefly with 45 Squadron but did not add to his score. He died in Vancouver in 1982.

Lieutenant Roy C. McLaren who served in 28 Squadron, seen here in his fur-lined flying overall. Note the large angled pocket on his chest, large enough to carry a map that would be easily accessible in flight.

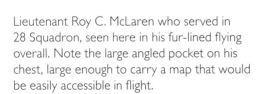

Chapter 5

The Battle of the Piave

When the British army occupied the Asiago sector, the original plan had been to attack the Austrians towards the Val Suguna. However, the situation in France caused a postponement, and instead it was the Austrians that took the offensive. Then, as the problem in France caused British troops to be withdrawn from the Italian front on the Piave River, the Camels began flying three-man patrols over both the Piave and Asiago areas to maintain a presence.

Enemy reconnaissance aircraft were constantly over allied positions and the Camels were flying barrage patrols between Fornia and Gallio. It was presumed that while the Austrians were preparing to attack, unknown to the allies they had changed their plan of advance to the Piave. In order to conceal their intentions, they were moving all men and equipment during the hours of darkness.

On the first day of June 45 Squadron lost one of its ace pilots – Earl Hand – to the Austro-Hungarian pilot Frank Linke-Crawford. Hand was on patrol along with Lieutenants Paddy O'Neill and J.P. 'Proc' Huins. Huins had this to say about the action in a letter to the author:

An early morning O.P., 6-7.15 am, over the lines. Paddy had engine trouble and returned to base before we crossed the lines. Hand and myself climbed to 12,000 feet flying east, with me on his starboard side. When some 7-10 miles over a sudden waggling of wings by Hand, indicated he had spotted some E.A. well below us. Down he went in a good dive and I followed on, flattening out after the dive. Hand immediately closed in combat with a black machine with a large camouflaged letter 'L' on the top of the centre section of his machine.

I was about 100 yards away and as I hurried on a parallel course, Hand turned out of the tight circle in which he and the E.A. was involved, and I saw flames come from Hand's main tank behind his back. The pilot of the 'L' machine was about 200 yards away. I turned towards him and we came head-on; he opened fire first and a second later I replied – a two-second burst but then both [my] guns jammed. I held my head-on approach and decided to fly for a collision. At the last moment when it seemed certain we would collide the E.A. went under, and he passed beneath me. I immediately did a steep left turn and came round inside the E.A., which was turning left. I finished some ten yards or less on his tail, the pilot looking over his left shoulder, then he half-rolled and went down vertically. I held my height as the E.A. flattened out at tree-top level, and flying 'on the carpet' went east.

I realised my engine was running rough as my Camel had been damaged in the encounter. The leading edge of my wings were torn and flapping in the breeze, the engine damaged, and the windmill pump on the right centre section strut had been shot away. I turned on to the gravity tank and limped back to our side of the lines, taking a last look at Hand's burning machine.

Earl Hand, from Ontario, was lucky to survive the encounter, crashing in flames. Although he suffered some burns, he got clear of the wreckage and soon found himself taken prisoner. He had gained five victories over France and Italy, and later received the DFC. 'Proc' Huins later became a doctor and spent a lot of time studying aviation medicine, for which he was made an OBE and received the Air Force Cross and Bar.

Two casualties in early June were Second Lieutenant A.F. Bartlett of 66 Squadron (B7353) taken prisoner on the 6th, and Lieutenant G.D. McLeod of 28 Squadron (B2316) wounded and captured on the 8th. He lingered until he succumbed to his injuries on 22 January 1919.

From 10 June 1918, Camels again began making their barrage patrols between Fornia and Gallio in order to restrict Austrian air reconnaissance over these areas; also what were termed 'long patrols' which were flown some 5 miles into enemy territory between Casotto and Cismon. Meanwhile, British and Italian air reconnaissance reports and photographs finally revealed that the Austrians were planning to attack the Piave sector. Austrian intentions, however, were not clear until a heavy bombardment began at 0300 hours on the 15th from the Adriatic coast to Astico. The Austrians also attacked Italian positions on the Piave, French positions on Mount Grappa and the remaining British forces on the Asiago plateau.

Low mist prevented any real air operations against the enemy offensive, especially over these mountainous regions. However, a patrol led by Spike Howell of 45 Squadron did manage to spot early signs of the attack. Austrian troops were crossing the Piave under cover of smoke screens, in boats and by erecting pontoon bridges. No. 45 Squadron then began sending out Camels in threes, dropping 20lb Cooper bombs on both these types of targets. The Camels then came in at low level to machine-gun targets of opportunity, causing many casualties among the assaulting soldiery. These attacks continued as the weather improved and in total, 45 Squadron alone flew thirty-five sorties dropping 112 x 20lb bombs plus another twenty bombs on Asiago targets. This was followed by an all-out attack by Camels and Bristol fighters of 'Z' Flight, the latter recently formed from C Flight of 34 Squadron, to help with recce sorties and based at Istrana. (In July it would become 139 Squadron.) Italian fighters and bombers also added to the Austrians' discomfort.

In all, during the initial assault by the Austrians, the RAF dropped 350 × 20lb bombs on the crossings. After dark, the Austrians began rebuilding destroyed or damaged pontoon bridges and also managed to get troops across in boats under cover of darkness. As dawn broke on the second day, ground mist again hampered early attempts by the RAF to engage them but as this began to lift around 0900, the Camels were once more causing mayhem.

Austrian and German aircraft were in evidence above these crossings, and British pilots had some success. On the 15th 28 Squadron claimed three Albatros fighters and two balloons, while 66, under Carpenter, shot down three: two Albatros D.Vs and a Brandenburg two-seater. In the meantime, 45 Squadron bagged four two-seaters, including one by the CO, Major A.M. Vaucour: a DFW in flames. Lieutenant S.W. Ellison was wounded on the 16th (B5204), later dying of his wounds. By the 16th the Austrians were in retreat.

On the 17th low cloud and rain grounded all aircraft, but the weather became the ultimate ruin of the Austrian offensive. These rains poured tons of water down from the mountains and into the river, sweeping away bridges and upsetting boats as the torrent raged. By 18 June only two bridges remained usable but it was the beginning of the end for the Austrians. The Italians now began a counter-attack and by the 19th the Austrians were in full retreat. Better weather allowed Camels to get into the action, 45 Squadron claiming eight enemy aircraft, two of these by Howell and three by Lieutenant J.H. Dewhirst. Bunny Vaucour destroyed another two-seater.

Cooper of 28 had downed one enemy machine on the 18th, while McEwen and Williams scored on the 19th; McEwen with one Berg fighter in flames and another 'ooc', Voss Williams a D.V crashed. On the 19th Lieutenant S.M. Robins of 28 was brought down by AA fire to become a prisoner (Camel D9310 'D').

A serious loss to Britain's Italian ally was that of Maggiore Francesco Baracca, their leading air ace with thirty-four victories. He had flown out on a ground strafing sortie on the 19th and failed to return. He was 30 years of age and had claimed his last two victories on 15 June.

At around 0900 hours on 21 June, Barker, Apps and Birks claimed three Albatros D.IIIs near Motta air base, located 10 miles east of the Piave. Barker and Birks had been flying together for some time, with Birks acting as his wingman; in fact, there had been nearly forty such flights and on this date, Gerry Birks made his twelfth and last claim. In the event it seems that only one Albatros was actually destroyed, with *Oberleutnant* F. Dechant of Flik 51J in 153.88 being killed. Barker had spotted a number of Austrian fighters taking off from Motta and decided to climb higher and to the north-east, biding his time till the hostiles were near Oderzo, closer to the front lines. Barker took his two partners in an arc so that the morning sun was behind them and then dived. Barker's fire sent one opponent down in a spin and then it broke up. Birks and 'Mable' Apps each sent opponents spinning earthwards. On the 22nd Eycott-Martin flamed a Brandenburg C-type over Arsie.

Gerry Birks had flown a total of sixty-six patrols over Italy by the 24th and was pretty tired, so was rested. It was not long before he was on a ship sailing home to Canada. He went on to live to the age of 96, although he never flew again. A banker, he married twice, had several children and died in Toronto in May 1991. Apart from Josef Kiss, Birks had also downed another Austrian ace, *Oberleutnant* Karl Patzelt on 4 May 1918, as mentioned earlier.

By the 24th, the Austrians had fallen back to their original positions at the start of the offensive, having incurred serious losses including some 20,000 men taken prisoner, those who had been unable to get back across the Piave. The RAF, especially the Camel squadrons, had played a significant part in this victory.

Combats continued to be had by all three Camel squadrons during the rest of June and into July. Cliff McEwen racked up eleven victories in these two months, bringing his score to twenty-four. Seven of these he scored flying D8112 but following one of these in this machine on 1 July, a Berg Scout, he crashed into trees near Isola di Cartura and was badly shaken. However, he was awarded the DFC, adding this to his earlier MC. He also received the Italian Bronze Medal. In the Second World War he commanded No. 6 (Canadian) Bomber Group in England from January 1944. He died in Toronto in 1967.

Lieutenant McEvoy, in D8235 'T', shot down a Pfalz Scout north-west of Asiago on 4 July and ten days later, in this same machine, he was forced to crash-land in a marsh following another combat. He was unhurt.

No. 28 Squadron lost Lieutenant A.R. Strang on 13 July (D8209) on a morning patrol. He was attacking a two-seater with two other pilots and although the enemy machine was claimed as destroyed, Strang sharing the kill with Joe Mackereth and Captain J.E. Hallonquist, he was missing after the fight, ending up as a prisoner.

***

On 3 July, the RAF's 'Z' Flight became 139 Squadron and command of it was given to Will Barker in mid-July. It was equipped with the BF2b – Bristol Fighter – a fighting machine that had already proved itself on the Western Front. Manned by an aggressive pilot and a competent observer/gunner, the 'Brisfit' was a formidable adversary for the enemy. Barker by this time had achieved thirty-eight victories. One amazing concession already given was to be allowed once again: that he could take his beloved Camel B6313 with him, despite his command flying two-seater Bristols. By this stage the two front wing struts of his Camel had white notches painted on them, one for each victory. When his Italian tour of duty ended in September, there would be forty-six notches. Incredibly he had scored all these victories in this aircraft, operating with it in France and Italy for almost a year. Some years ago this author saw this Camel's log book, retained in the Imperial War Museum, London.

What Barker thought of this posting can only be imagined, but at least he could continue flying his beloved Camel. Before mid-September, he added a further seven victories to his score and was then posted back to England. As is well known, he managed to wangle a posting back to France, arguing that he needed to be brought 'up to speed' on operations over France, and went to 201 Squadron, flying the new Sopwith Snipes.

On 27 October he fought a number of enemy aircraft in a one-man scrap, and although badly wounded he was credited with four victories before being forced to crash-land. For this he was awarded the Victoria Cross.

***

By far the most serious loss to the Camel squadrons in Italy was the death of 45 Squadron's CO, Major Awdry Morris Vaucour MC & Bar, DFC and the Italian Silver Medal for Military Valour (*Medaglia d'Argento al Valore Militare*). His penchant for often flying over the front on his own finally cost him his life.

On 16 July he was flying Camel D8102, keeping an eye out for his squadron's patrols across the front lines. There are two versions of what happened; the British one believing that Vaucour, having spotted an aircraft and realizing that it was Italian, had tried to reassure its pilot he was friendly by flying in front so that the pilot could recognize the British roundels. However, the Italian pilot reported seeing an aircraft heading towards him, and being at around 0900 hours, the low sun was blinding him. He believed he could see black crosses on it and as it passed, he turned and dived to the attack, firing as he came within range.

Too late, he saw that it was a British machine but his fire had already hit Vaucour, the wounded pilot diving some distance before the Camel began to disintegrate, the wreckage falling near Monastier di Treviso. The Italian pilot was Lieutenant Alberto Moresco in a Hanriot scout of the 78ª *Squadriglia*. Bunny Vaucour was 28 years old, the son of a vicar, born in Topcliffe, Yorkshire. He had claimed five victories over Italy plus three more in France.

Gordon Apps of 66 Squadron was wounded by AA fire over Belluno in B7358 on the 17th. He had gained his tenth and final victory before this event, sharing an LVG two-seater destroyed with Lieutenant A.E. Baker. Apps was later awarded the DFC.

On 27 July, Major J.A.H. Crook MC arrived from England and took command of 45 Squadron. Amazing as it sounds, Joe Crook was only 21 years of age and had won his MC in 1916, aged just 18, on two-seater corps aircraft. One might have expected one of the experienced Camel pilots in Italy to have been promoted to this command.

The Austro-Hungarians also lost one of their leading pilots on 31 July. *Oberleutnant* Frank Linke-Crawford had downed his 29th victory two days earlier, a BF2b of 139 Squadron. In recent weeks he had also claimed four Camels, with both 28 and 45 Squadrons suffering losses. Flying a Berg D.I, he tangled with 45 Squadron and had to spin down out of trouble and damaged, but then ran into two Italian fighters. Unable to manoeuvre properly, he fell to the guns of Corporal Aldo Astolfi of the 81ª *Squadriglia*, the latter's first and only combat success.

Upon hearing that Linke-Crawford had been killed, RAF HQ quickly tried to establish whether an RAF pilot had got him and soon discovered that 45 Squadron had been in action that morning, also that Lieutenant Jack Cottle had claimed a victory. At first it was thought that Cottle should be credited; indeed, he was told so by Colonel Joubert de la Ferté who had telephoned 45 Squadron asking that Cottle should come to his HQ. In his own recollections, Cottle said that the machine he shot down was a new type with red and green stripes along its fuselage and a large octagonal 'C'. Cottle, along with Charles Catto and Francis Bowles, had been in a scrap with enemy fighters and the latter two pilots confirmed seeing Cottle's opponent going down. In 45's game book Cottle's record page has even had reference to Linke-Crawford being the victim, the fighter falling in pieces over Fontane.

However, other evidence seems to indicate that Cottle had shot down a Phönix D.I flown by *Feldwebel* J. Acs of Flik 60J. The difficulty is that Acs appears to have made a forced landing, his machine badly damaged, so not falling to pieces in the air. The Phönix was not a new type at the front, and photos of Linke-Crawford's machine – a Berg, serial number 115.32 – show a large 'L' on the fuselage. The Italian pilot had reported his victim crashing in flames and he had received confirmation from a nearby artillery observation post. Other pictures show that Flik 60J carried octagonal letters on their machines, such as Kurt Gruber's 'G'.

Linke-Crawford was in fact engaged by Italian Hanriots and shot down in flames after a long combat with 81ª Squadriglia, Corporal Aldo Astolfi claiming his first and only victory as stated above.

***

August 1918 saw a continuation of the fighting in the air. No. 45 Squadron made a total of twenty-two claims, sixteen noted as destroyed. No. 66 Squadron also put in claims for twenty-two, all but one as being destroyed. No. 28 Squadron only claimed four, three being destroyed. All suffered losses.

No. 45 Squadron lost Lieutenant A.L. Haines DFC on the 10th. Alf Haines came from Evesham, Worcs, a pre-war farmer, and two victories on 29 July had brought his score to six. His DFC was announced after his death. He was very unlucky to be hit by an anti-aircraft shell while flying at 10,000ft, falling in no man's land from where enemy troops carried his body to the British lines under a white flag.

The other two losses were both results of flying accidents, with Captain W.C. Hilborn DFC losing his life. Canadian Bill Hilborn had attained seven victories and again his DFC was announced after his death on 16 August. He had flown with 66, 28 and finally as a flight commander in 45 two days prior to his crash, although he lingered on for ten days before dying.

No. 28 Squadron only suffered one loss in August with Lieutenant S. Yates being injured in a crash, but 66 Squadron had three casualties. On the 5th, Lieutenant G.C. Easton (B6354) was lost on a patrol and reported killed. Lieutenant E.P. O'Connor-Glynn died following a flying accident on the 17th in B2433, while Captain J. Mackereth (E1496) failed to return on the 31st. However, John Mackereth from Essex survived as a prisoner. Most of his time in Italy had been spent with 28 Squadron until being made a flight commander with 66. However, his tour with them did not last long, for while attacking and destroying a balloon he was hit in the leg by ground fire, crashed and was taken captive. He had gained seven victories.

Another successful 66 Squadron pilot was C.M. Maud from Leeds, formerly with the Royal Field Artillery. Charles Maud celebrated his 22nd birthday on the day the RAF was formed: 1 April 1918. He had been with 66 since March but finally got into his stride during May, with five victories that month. By 23 August he had raised this to ten and number eleven came on 7 October. He was awarded the DFC and the Italian *Croce di Guerra*.

Air fighting diminished during September, although patrols were still flown across the Asiago front. RAF Intelligence Reports indicated to RAF HQ that the Austro-Hungarian Air Corps were in poor shape, and bad weather over northern Italy did not help either side. Following the massive German offensive in France, it was thought at one stage that much of the British force in Italy might need to return to the Western Front and indeed, nine army battalions were sent during the summer.

Also going back to France was 45 Squadron, and they fought their last air actions on 31 August. In early September the squadron began to dismantle its aircraft and prepare to leave. Once they returned they were attached to Hugh Trenchard's Independent Force, tasked with bombing French and German strategic targets. Although the squadron was there to give protection, its fighters saw little action until the last weeks of the war, mainly against German reconnaissance aircraft.

The pilots of 28 Squadron managed to get into several combats, but it was mostly new pilots who began to claw down the odd victim or two. Stan Stanger and Cliff McEwen both added to their already impressive scores as the war over Italy gradually came to an end. Stanger, from Montreal, was a flight commander with 28 after initially being with 66. His last three victories in September and October brought his score to thirteen, and he added the DFC to his earlier MC. McEwen, from Manitoba, brought his score to twenty-seven during the last weeks of the war, and had also been awarded the MC and DFC. One of his claims, for an Albatros D.III on 18 February 1918, was only credited as an 'ooc' victory, but some years later the wreckage was discovered in the mountains which raised his credit to 'destroyed'.

No. 66 Squadron, on the other hand, got into numerous combats and during September and October gained an impressive thirty-one claims. Among these pilots was Lieutenant H.K. Goode.

Harry King Goode, from Handsworth and formerly a Royal Engineer, had achieved seven victories by August 1918, but in the last weeks he downed seven more, the last six being kite balloons. One of these fell on 29 October, after which he attacked the enemy airfield at South Gioncomo, claiming three enemy aircraft destroyed on the ground. He ended the war with the DFC and then the DSO. He remained in the RAF after the war, becoming a group captain, but was killed in a flying accident, as a passenger, in August 1942.

***

With the war on the Western Front going well, it was hoped that in northern Italy the Austro-Hungarian forces would also soon be defeated. One British division remained on the Asiago plateau, but the other two had joined up with the American and French units who were supporting the Italians on the Piave front. To allay suspicions, British soldiers took to wearing Italian uniforms, while all flying operations were kept to the Asiago front.

The opening push began on 4 and 5 October with two air-raids on Austrian advanced training schools. Twenty-three Camels from 28 and 66 attacked Campoformido with high-explosive and phosphorus bombs, and a few enemy machines that tried to interfere were engaged, one being claimed by Stanger and McEwen. The next day Egna in the Adige Valley received attention from twenty-two Camels. No. 28 Squadron had two pilots shot down on the 4th – Lieutenant J.H.R. Bryant killed in B5638 and Lieutenant A. Latimer killed in D8244 – while Lieutenant R.H. Foss shot down an LVG two-seater on the 5th. No. 28 Squadron also had a pilot wounded on the 5th: Second Lieutenant C.S. Styles in E1581.

On the 7th *Oberleutnant* Ludwig Hautzmeyer of Flik 61J shot down Camel D8215 of 66 Squadron flown by Lieutenant W.J. Courtney, his sixth victory, and *Oberleutnant* Franz Peter of Flik 3J downed another (E1498) flown by Second Lieutenant G.R. Leighton, a 26-year-old Scot from Glasgow, also his sixth victory. Further operations were begun on 23 October, followed by more decisive action on the 27th. Allied troops crossed the Piave, attacked by the Austrians from the air, while Camels went for the enemy's balloon lines, three being shot down by 66 Squadron. Enemy forces, once allied soldiers had got across the river, were in retreat.

Augustus Paget from Wiltshire gained all his six victories in these last weeks in Italy with 66 Squadron and was awarded the DFC. However, his luck ran out on 30 October, being brought down and killed by ground fire.

Austrian forces tried to counter the offensive on the 29th but they were finally broken, with low-flying Camels constantly ground-strafing and bombing Austrian ground forces. Over the next few days much carnage was done to the enemy troops from the air, as the allied soldiers constantly pushed forward. The Armistice in Italy finally came into effect on 4 November 1918.

Camel B5181 'C' of 45 Squadron, summer 1918. Flown by Jack Cottle, Francis Bowles and M. Gibson, it accounted for five enemy aircraft. Note its serial number is painted on the fin twice.

Five 66 Squadron pilots. Front: William MacDonald DFC from Vancouver, eight victories; Peter Carpenter DSO, MC, twenty-four victories with 45 and 66; Alfred Bartlett DFC, five victories, PoW 6 June. Rear: R.G. Reid, three victories, and T.H. Timmis, three victories.

Major A.M. Vaucour MC & Bar, DFC, Italian *Medaglia d'Argento al Valore Militare*. Commanding officer of 45 Squadron, shot down and killed by 'friendly fire' on 16 July 1918.

A Hanriot scout, the type that shot down Bunny Vaucour. This particular machine was being flown by Italian ace Silvio Scaroni when he was shot down on 12 July 1918; badly wounded, he did not see further action.

Captain C.E. Howell DSO, MC, DFC of 45 Squadron. Cedric 'Spike' Howell achieved nineteen victories over Italy between January and July 1918. From Adelaide, Australia, he had earlier served in Egypt and Gallipoli before transferring to become a pilot. Sadly he was drowned off Corfu in 1919, attempting a flight from England to Australia.

Above: A line-up of BF2b fighters of 139 Squadron. Captain W.G. Barker of 66 Squadron was promoted to command this unit, formerly known as 'Z' Flight in Italy, but he was allowed to take with him his famous Camel that he had flown exclusively since October 1917 with both 28 and 66 Squadrons.

Below: Barker's Camel, B6313, while with 139 Squadron. On the tailfin one can see a red heart pierced by a white arrow, and on the right-hand Vickers gun there is a red devil thumbing its nose towards the enemy.

Billy Barker revving up the engine of B6313. On the two front wing struts one can just make out tiny white painted notches, one for each of his victories. The tail of a 139 BF2b is off to the right. In all Barker had claimed forty-six victories in this machine; a record not only for a Camel, but for any aircraft in the First World War

Barker flying his Camel over the Italian landscape. Note the amount of engine exhaust flowing back in the slipstream.

Captain Jack Cottle DFC of 45 Squadron. From Plymouth, Devon, he spent his early years in Zululand and before joining the RFC had served with the South African Mounted Rifles. His victory score of thirteen included three enemy machines that were brought down on the allied side of the lines. Eleven of his claims were over Italy, the last two when back in France in November 1918. He received the DFC and the Italian *Medaglia d'Argento* (Silver) *al Valore Militare.*

Captain Clifford McEwen MC, DFC, Italian *Medaglia di Bronzo al Valore Militare*. With twenty-seven victories, he was 28 Squadron's top scorer. Serving with the RCAF after the war, he rose to air vice marshal and in the Second World War commanded No. 6 (Canadian) Bomber Group in England. The Camel pictured here is one decorated after the First World War and in which he scored four of his victories. Note the unusual painting of the serial number.

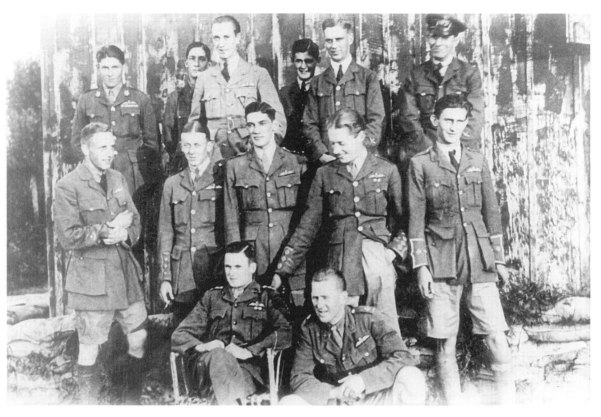

Pilots of 28 Squadron in August 1918. Back row:
C.M. McEwen; S. Yates; A.F. White; unknown; E.J. Ffolken-
Jones; E.F. Mattock. Middle row: R.H. Foss; J.E. Hallonquist;
W.C. Hilborn; Major O.M. Sutton (CO); G.S. Style. Front
row: S. Stanger; R.C. McLaren.

Another elaborately-painted Camel after the war.
The picture clearly shows the Aldis gun-sight and the
petrol windmill pump on the starboard strut.

A 66 Squadron
Camel, coded 'S',
October 1918.

A group of 45 Squadron pilots, c. August 1918. L to R: Charles Catto; Mansell R. James; J.R. Black; Francis
S. Bowles; H.T. Doc Smith (USAS, MO); A. Rice-Oxley. James was lost in 1919 while flying one of the
first Camels to be flown in America. He became lost over dense forests and was never seen again.

Above left: Harry King Goode, DSO, DFC from Handsworth scored fifteen victories with 66 Squadron, including seven kite balloons. He died as a group captain as a passenger in a B24 Liberator of Coastal Command in the Second World War.

Above right: Captain C.M. Maud DFC. Yorkshireman Charles Maud scored eleven victories with 66 Squadron over Italy and was rewarded with the DFC and the Italian War Cross. Beneath his RAF wings is the early DFC ribbon before the stripes became diagonal.

Opposoite: Lieutenant A.J. Haines from Evesham, Worcs claimed six victories with 45 Squadron before his death on 10 August 1918.

Sopwith Camel E1502 of 28 Squadron, coded 'J' and with the squadron's white square identification marking. The pilot is Captain R.H. Foss, who shot down two Austrian aircraft while flying it, a share in an Albatros D.III on 15 September and an LVG two-seater on 5 October.

Roy H. Foss of 28 Squadron.

Lieutenant J.S. Lennox of 66 Squadron claimed three victories in 1918.

Oberleutnant Franz Peter of Flik 3J shot down Second Lieutenant G.R. Leighton of 66 Squadron on 7 October 1918 for his sixth victory.

Oberleutnant Ludwig Hautzmeyer of Flik 61J shot down Lieutenant W.J. Courtney of 66 Squadron on 7 October 1918, his sixth victory. Hautzmeyer was killed in an air crash at London's Croydon Airport in 1936.

A Sopwith Camel (E7167) of 66 Squadron following a forced landing. Lieutenant J.M. Kelly MM had been brought down by Flik 30 on 22 October 1918 and taken prisoner. Rather than the white bar markings of 28 on the fuselage, it carries the dumbbells of 45 Squadron, believed to be a ruse to confuse the enemy about 45 having left Italy for France.

Oberleutnant Franz Rudorfer was with Flik F51J in 1918, claiming a total of eleven victories including Camels. On 7 October he shared one with *Feldwebel* Eugen Bönsch and two on 27 October, one being from 28 Squadron, which he forced to land. Rudorfer died in the influenza epidemic in 1919.

Left: Captain C.E. 'Spike' Howell DSO, MC, DFC; nineteen victories with 45 Squadron. He was drowned attempting a flight from England to Australia on 10 December 1919. A veteran of Gallipoli, he was 23 years old.

Below: Pilots of 66 Squadron on 1 October 1918. Back row: Lieutenants E.D. Salthouse; S.J. Osborne; Carmichael. Next row: Lieutenants F.W. Higgins; A. Paget (KIA 30 October); J.W. Bishop; W.J. Courtney (PoW 7 October); unknown; unknown; J.S. Lennox; unknown; unknown. Seated: Lieutenant W.M. MacDonald; Captain C.M. Maud; unknown; Captain P. Carpenter; Major J.T. Whittaker; Lieutenant N.S. Taylor; Captain H.K. Goode; Captain J.M. Warnock. Front left: Lieutenants A.J. Howell; A.E. Baker; R.G. Reid. Front right: not identified.

Opposite above: A few of 28 Squadron in late 1918. L to R: Italian officer; Lieutenants E.F. Muttock; C.G. Constandious; F.T. Everett; R.B. Beever. Everett, Beever and Muttock downed a Halberstadt C-type on 15 September, while Constandious destroyed an Albatros D.V on 25 October.

Opposite below: Pilots and ground crew of 45 Squadron back in France. Seated: Lieutenants J.C. Williams; C.W. Verity; M. Gibson; C.G. Catto; Captain J. Cottle DFC; A.F. Lingard; L.B. Irish; G. Exley. Cottle claimed the squadron's final victory over Italy on 31 August and scored twice more over France in the last days of the war.

Appendix

Sopwith Camel Aces Over Italy

Key: Sqns = Squadrons; Dest = Destroyed; OOC = Out of control; KBs = Kite balloons.

NAME	SQNS	DEST	OOC	KBs	WAR TOTAL
Barker, Capt. W.G.	28 66 139	12 14 6	1 2 2	9	 50
McEwen, Capt. C.M.	28	23	4		27
Carpenter, Capt. P.	45 66	7 12	1 4	- -	 24
Frew, Capt. M.B.	45	6	1		23
Howell, Capt. C.E.	45	16	3		19
Goode, Lt. H.K.	66	6	1	8	15
Williams, Capt. T.F.	45 28	2 5	2 1	-	 14
Cottle, Capt. J.	45	11	2		13
Hudson, Lt. H.B.	28	4	2	7	13
Stanger, Capt. S.	66 28	2 10	1 -		 13
Symondson, Capt. F.S.	66	10	1	2	13
Birks, Lt. G.A.	66	12			12
Brownell, Capt. R.J.	45	5	1	1	12
Montgomery, Capt. K.B.	45 66	1 1		-	 12
Firth, Capt. J.C.B.	45	1	1	-	11
Maud, Capt. C.M.	66	8	3		11
Mitchell, Capt. J.H.	28	8			11

NAME	SQNS	DEST	OOC	KBs	WAR TOTAL
Apps, Lt. G.F.M.	66	8	2		10
Bell, Capt. H.B.	66	8	2		10
Dawes, Capt. R.J.	45 28	4 1	4	-	9
Jones, Capt. N.C.	28 45	1 7	1		9
McEvoy, Lt. C.	66	7	2		9
Eycott-Martin, Lt. H.R.	66	8			8
MacDonald, Lt. W.M.	66	8			8
Masters, Lt. E.H.	45	6	2		8
Moody, Lt. H.M.	45	3	1		8
Cooper, Lt. A.G.	28	5	1	-	7
Dewhirst, Lt. J.H.	45	6	1		7
Hilborn, Capt. W.C.	66 28	6 1			7
Jerrard, Lt. A.	66	5	1	1	7
Wilson, Capt. P.	28	6	-	1	7
Mackereth, Capt. J.	28 66	5	1	1	7
Vaucour, Maj. A.M.	45	3	1		7
Catto, Lt. C.G.	45	4	2		6
Haines, Lt. A.J.	45	6			6
Paget, Lt. A.	66	3	2	1	6
Rice-Oxley, Lt. A.	45	4	2		6
Bowles, Lt. F.S.	45	4	1		5
Boyson, Lt. H.K.	66	4	1		5
Child, Lt. J.E.	45	2			5
Hallonquist, Capt. J.E.	28	5			5
Hand, Lt. E. McN.	45	4			5
Jarvis, Lt. A.G.	28	3	1	1	5

Where the war totals differ from claims made over Italy, they include victories claimed either while over France before going to Italy, or over France after their return, or while serving with other squadrons prior to postings to 28, 45 or 66 Squadrons.